INCREASING REVENUE FROM YOUR CLIENTS

DICK CONNOR, C.M.C.

WILEY

John Wiley & Sons

New York • Chichester • Brisbane • Toronto • Singapore

Published by John Wiley & Sons, Inc.

Library of Congress Cataloging-in-Publication Information

ISBN 0-471-62052-1

Printed in the United States of America

10 9 8 7 6 5 4 3 2 1

PREFACE

This book is about creating profitable revenue from your existing clients. It also covers the increasingly important task of protecting revenue obtained from existing clients that may either be targeted by more aggressive firms or be deemed vulnerable because of changes in the primary client-firm relationship.

The book is a logical extension of my first two books, *Marketing Your Consulting and Professional Services* and *Getting New Clients*. Although this book follows the other two, the three need not be read in sequence. *Increasing Revenue from Your Clients* assumes no prior understanding of Client-Centered Marketing[*] on the part of the reader, and I have conceived it as a stand-alone book that the intelligent reader can approach without inhibition.

Interested readers may, however, want to refer to my earlier books to gain greater insight into some of the concepts touched on in this book. *Marketing Your Consulting and Professional*

Services provides a broad-gauged overview of client-centered marketing. *Getting New Clients* is an in-depth analysis of the art and science of "nichemanship."

[*]Note: Client-Centered Marketing™ is my sole property.

Acknowledgments

This book is an outgrowth of the insights I have gained in serving hundreds of clients worldwide. In writing it I have profited from the advice, criticism, and support received from my clients and others who are eager to see this book succeed. My gratitude goes out to them.

Particular thanks go to my editor, John B. Mahaney, who had the good sense to focus my vision on existing clients, rather than on the broader-based subject matter I originally envisioned. The result, I believe, is a product that will be more beneficial to the professional practitioner.

Tim Wells, a noted writer in his own right, sharpened my prose. His insights and labor were vital at every stage of manuscript development.

And finally, my acknowledgment to Susan, who again provided the space and support for this book to be completed.

D.C.

About the Author

Dick Connor's service marketing consulting practice serves the accounting, consulting and public relations professions world-wide. He is a certified management consultant, CMC.

The originator of the Client-Centered Marketing™ system, he specializes in assisting firms in designing and installing marketing programs and personal selling programs that focus initially on serving and retaining their present clients.

One of the two books Dick has coauthored with Jeffrey Davidson, *Getting New Clients* (John Wiley & Sons, 1987), is already in its third printing. The *Library Journal* designated this book as "The Best in Business Writing in 1987." An audio tape version of this book is available through Wiley Sound Business cassettebooks. His first book, *Marketing Your Consulting and Professional Services* (John Wiley & Sons, 1985) is now in its seventh printing.

Formerly an Associate Professor of Management at Northwestern Graduate School of Management, Dick was also a contributing author in the *Encyclopedia of Professional Management*. Elected to the National Small Business Development Center (SBDC) Advisory Board, he is listed in the Southwest and International editions of *Who's Who in Business and the Professions*.

Dick lives with his wife Susan in Springfield, Virginia.

CONTENTS

The great virtue of Client-centered Marketing (tm)[1] is that it dispenses with myths and half-truths that equate marketing largely with external activities such as promotion, glad-handing, buy-ins, advertising, sharp pricing, and other hard-sell techniques.

A client-centered marketing approach cuts straight to the hard reality of the business world: *Marketing and client service are interdependent and mutually reinforcing.* Herein lies the key to understanding how you can create additional revenue, develop referrals, and make your practice more profitable.

You may, quite naturally, ask: What is client-centered marketing? And how can I learn to apply its principles and tools in serving my clients? These are important questions. The goal of this chapter is to answer the first question. To do so, I will define client-centered marketing, examine the four-element client-centered marketing system, and discuss two essential concepts: leveraging and marketing comfort zone. The remaining chapters of the book are devoted to answering the second question. In defining client-centered market-

[1]Client-centered Marketing is a trademark for a marketing orientation that puts the needs and expectations of clients and prospective clients first in the client–firm relationship. Need satisfaction, not the selling of a service, is the primary focus of the professional.

1

The Client-Centered Marketing Approach

Since forming my services marketing consulting practice in 1970, I have had the privilege of serving close to 500 professional and consulting firms of all sizes, worldwide.

My experience in working with these dedicated professionals shows that there is a fortune to be made by "mining the gold in one's own back yard": The current client base of the typical service provider can be a private, captive market that is waiting to be cultivated and harvested. But I have also discovered that many service providers tend to think of marketing as a task that can be ignored in existing client-firm relationships. One veteran consultant confided recently, "Once the thrill of the hunt is over, and the prospect is now a client, my focus turns to getting more new clients."

It is not uncommon for a service-oriented professional—such as a consultant, attorney, engineer, or accountant—to view marketing primarily as an *external* activity, the sole function of which is to entice new clients to purchase the firm's services.

Such an assumption can be detrimental to profitable growth in today's increasingly competitive environment. It undermines the development and maintenance of sound client–firm relationships, and often causes professionals to overlook opportunities for generating additional revenues and referrals from their most desirable clients.

ing, this chapter lays the foundation for the rest of the book.

CLIENT-CENTERED MARKETING

At its most basic level, client-centered marketing is the strategic decision to develop a special type of client–firm relationship with your most desirable clients in your targeted industries. It is not for every client you serve, only for those that you deem worth the investment. Once this special relationship is established, the primary and continuing task is to sense, sell, serve, and satisfy the needs and expectations of these clients in mutually profitable ways. Your desirable clients are identified as the primary targets and beneficiaries of your time, talent, and specialized technology.

In putting client-centered marketing into practice, your goal is relationship and revenue enhancement. But it is revenue enhancement that is intimately tied to client satisfaction, not based on advertising or promotion. The cultivation of a satisfied client requires more than a job well done. It requires the building of a *value-added relationship*. To build this relationship, you need to understand your client's business and industry, goals, needs, and areas of potential growth. In addition, you need to *create* opportunities to put this knowledge into practice. Chapter 3 will show you how to build these special relationships.

Services marketing is an evolving discipline, and years of experience has taught me that terms such as *markets* and *niches* are often misused, or even used interchangeably by practitioners in the field. This can lead to unnecessary confusion. In order to avoid any misunderstanding, I will define a number of essential marketing terms as I discuss the client-centered marketing system.

THE CLIENT-CENTERED MARKETING SYSTEM

The client-centered marketing system, shown in Exhibit 1-1, is made up of four basic elements: existing practice factors; existing referral sources; targets of opportunity, attention, concern, and influence; and new business development factors. A careful examination of each of these elements is necessary to develop an understanding of the system and to devise a workable plan for classifying your clients and sensing the needs of targeted clients. I will discuss the contents of each of these four elements and show their relationships to each other. You will be able to see how each element can influence the building, or disintegration, of the primary client–firm relationship.

Existing Practice Factors

The first element comprises eight different factors, each of which impacts on your current

Client satisfaction is crucial to growth and revenue enhancement, but satisfied clients are by no means equal. Every client–firm relationship is unique, and each possesses a different level of potential growth.

Your existing clients can be broadly classified in one of three ways: *desirable, unknown potential at this time,* or *undesirable.*

- *Desirable* clients produce good fees; some make referrals on your behalf, and others present opportunities for providing additional profitable services.

- *Unknown potential* clients are those whom you have not yet served, or are serving now for the first time, and have not yet classified in terms of their potential for growth or trouble.

- *Undesirable* clients include current desirable clients who may be targeted by other firms and those giving warning signals such as complaints about service. They also include those clients who represent fee and/or discount problems, and those few clients found in every practice that cause one to be sorry one accepted them in the first place.

These three broad categories represent a macro classification. Chapter 2 will show you how to further classify your existing clients into a micro system that categorizes them according to their potential for growth as well as their potential for trouble.

Industries Served

An industry is a group of similar organizations and individuals that address the same general needs of their clients and customers through their goods and services. Each industry is characterized by a four-digit Standard Industrial Code (SIC) number. The SIC is a classification system used to identify businesses by common industry groupings. Appendix A discusses the SIC system and lists sources of SIC information.

For our marketing purposes, an industry is composed of existing clients, prospective clients, "suspects," and known and need-to-know referral sources. *Suspects* are potential clients in your practice area whom you have not yet contacted.

The industries you serve represent different potentials for your firm.

- A *primary industry* is one in which the revenues produced by all your clients in the SIC constitute a large percentage of your total revenue, usually in excess of 10 to 15 percent.

- A *secondary industry* is one in which the revenue produced by all your clients in the

SIC constitutes a small percentage of your total revenue.

Your Markets

Your markets are the geographic areas (ZIP codes) in which you promote and conduct your business.

In nonservice marketing, the term *market* is used to define what Philip Kotler calls "a potential arena for the trading of resources." He also defines market as "the set of all actual and potential buyers of a product."

These definitions miss the mark for service marketers. Once we have identified our industry players using the SIC approach, we need to determine where these clients and prospects congregate, and where the largest number are in order to *leverage* our time, talents, and technology (the concept of leveraging will be discussed a bit later in this chapter).

I define market as: *the geographic area(s) in which you have chosen to promote and provide a particular service.* Next, I'll show you how this definition is used to define a targeted industry-market niche.

Your Targeted Industry-Market Niches

A niche is a targeted SIC-ZIP area on which you focus your time, talent, and technology. Your ongoing task is to identify and penetrate high-potential niches by recognizing and meeting the needs of high-potential clients and prospects with high-margin service solutions. My book *Getting New Clients* (Wiley, 1987) presents a client-centered approach to the art and science of *nichemanship*.

In the client-centered marketing system a niche is defined as: *A targeted SIC-ZIP(s) area on which you consciously choose to focus your attention and invest your relatively scarce and inexpensive time, talent, and technology for the purpose of penetrating, deepening, and eventually dominating the niche.* Your goal in nicheing is to become a major or dominant player in the niche. This requires focus, determination, and specialization.

For example, I currently serve the following SIC industry areas.

SIC	Description
8931A	Certified Public Accountants
7392A	Management Consultants
8911	Consulting Engineers
7361	Executive Search Consultants
7392	Public Relations Counselors

My targeted niches at this time are the following.

SIC	Description	ZIPs/Countries
8931A	Certified Public Accountants	All U.S. ZIPs

SIC	Description	ZIPs/Countries
7392A	Management Consultants	United States, Canada, and Australia
7392	Public Relations Counselors	ZIPS 20000 (Washington, DC area)

Your Services

There are four ways to classify your services.

- *Type I services* are services that your clients need but are often not happy about having to pay for. Services such as accounting, actuarial, employee benefits, auditing, and tax compliance are often viewed by clients as necessary evils.

- *Type II services* are both needed and wanted by your clients. These services include consultations such as cash flow planning, marketing strategy, and business reorganization, as well as other services that clients see as assisting them in operating and improving their business and competitive situation.

- *Type III services* are what I call fad, or "in," services. Such services might include developing computer templates for making important business decisions or providing advice about balloon mortgage financing.

- *Type IV services* are the high-margin, value-perceived consultations that are offered to high-potential clients and prospective clients in a targeted niche. Value-perceived consultations often result in value-billings, that is, billings that exceed the actual number of hours dedicated to producing the solution.

Your Technology

The term *technology* refers to the databases, engagement procedures, software applications, support systems, and the like, used in both marketing and providing client service. Properly developed and used, technology support systems reduce costs, increase productivity, and provide a competitive edge while strengthening your marketing comfort zone.

Your Personnel

You will want to classify your professionals in terms of *finder*, *minder*, or *grinder* status.

- Finders are the professionals who have a talent for uncovering needs, and who are willing to contact clients and prospective clients for the purpose of discussing services designed to meet a need or solve a problem.
- Minders are good at maintaining and enhancing relationships with existing clients. They also contribute to the development of value-perceived solutions by ensuring that the technical aspects of the solution are in place.

- Grinders are all the other professionals, who are more comfortable in the "doing" aspects of their profession. The beauty of the client-centered marketing approach is that the grinders are able to participate in marketing on their terms. In other marketing approaches, *grinder* is a negative term. Later chapters describe various marketing tools that can be used by these talented but more technically oriented professionals.

Existing Referral Sources

The second element in the marketing model contains two classes of referral sources: existing clients and non-client influentials.

Existing Clients

Clients who are especially satisfied with the range and quality of the services you provide frequently refer you to their friends. They can also provide you with leads, give written testimonials, and involve you in their professional and trade association activities, thus providing you with a valuable forum for building additional relationships. Clients who make referrals on your behalf provide you with leverage opportunities, so your relationship with them must be developed and protected.

Non-client Influentials

Non-client influentials include attorneys, bankers, editors, executive directors of industry associations, community leaders, and others who serve your clients in noncompetitive ways or influence their decisions regarding your type of services. These professionals are familiar with your firm and will frequently provide you with leads and introductions to prospective clients and other non-client influentials.

Of the four major elements in the client-centered marketing system, the two discussed thus far—existing practice factors and existing referral relationships—form the bedrock of your current practice. It is here that you live and work and have your billable hours.

Both elements reside within your current marketing comfort zone—that area in which you can comfortably and confidently initiate new business discussions with existing clients who need and want your services.

Targets of Opportunity, Attention, Concern, and Influence

The third element in the client-centered marketing system identifies four classes of targets that will help you prioritize your marketing time.

Targets of Opportunity for Additional Fees and Referrals

- Existing desirable clients who have additional needs, a sizable budget, and a willingness to discuss your proposed solutions with them.

17

Nonservice marketing approaches use the term "prospects" to refer to those out there who could, and should, buy your offering. I prefer a more realistic approach to this activity.

Earlier I defined a prospect as a non-client with whom you have had a potential new business discussion, but have not yet converted into a client with a firm business agreement.

Prospecting is the process of identifying high-potential suspect organizations in your markets and niches, and then contacting decision makers within those organizations to discuss a solution for a need they have. The goal of client-centered service marketers is to clone their most profitable desirable clients. Effective prospecting enables you to find and target non-clients who may ultimately become your most desirable new clients. Once a decision maker in a targeted suspect firm agrees to meet with you, he becomes a prospect.

New Business Discussions

Many authors refer to business discussions and selling calls. To me this implies a "telling," or "pushing the product," approach. In services marketing, selling is actually a directed discussion for the purpose of discovering if the contact has a need you can meet in mutually beneficial and desirable ways.

These discussions are conducted to discover and define a need situation with a target of opportunity, and to suggest a solution that involves contracting for your services.

The Concept of Leveraging

In addition to the four elements of the client-centered marketing system, two principles are put to work to ensure maximum efficiency and the potential for success. The first principle, *leveraging*, refers to the process of employing the smallest number of targeted actions, resources, and relationships to produce the greatest results. Leveraging is getting a disproportionate return on your investment of time, talent, and technology. Your return is revenue, referrals, and employment-niche experience. Leveraging is used to isolate, educate, relate to, and serve desirable clients in mutually beneficial ways.

The client-centered marketing approach firmly embraces the concept of leveraging as a necessary guide to time and resource management. Good results can be obtained by focusing your attention in appropriate ways on your current priority targets.

Leveraging is such an important notion and acquired skill that I want to present several examples to illustrate its dynamics.

- Visiting a banker to discuss the possibility of obtaining a referral or making a "vouch-for" response, and then finding out the names of attorneys he or she has a high regard for, is an example of leveraging your time with a *cascade* effect.

- Making a speech and arranging to have it tape-recorded enables you to market the tape, edit the remarks, and prepare articles and workbook sections.

- I try to take a four-mile walk every morning. During this time I listen to tapes of my recent speeches and also carry a small tape recorder to capture new ideas generated by listening to my remarks from a new perspective. I pay especially close attention to my improvised responses to questions from the audience (many of which I have "planted" earlier to ensure a favorable forum for my remarks; I simply ask my friends who will attend to be certain to ask me certain tough questions so I can demonstrate my mastery).

Working from Your Marketing Comfort Zone

When speaking before groups, I frequently refer to the fact that I am a scuba diver. My current comfort zone in diving is about 50 to 60 feet. I can dive to 90 or 100 feet, and on occasion have done so, but I am not comfortable. I get little joy out of it, and can't wait to get out of the water. This happens whenever I progress beyond the limits of my current comfort zone. The same is true in marketing.

The second principle of the client-centered marketing approach is that you should always work within your marketing comfort zone, which you can expand gradually. If, when you are developing new business and serving new clients, you move outside your comfort zone too quickly, the discomfort may be so great that you begin to withdraw and fall back to business as usual. To effectively increase the size of your comfort zone, you must move slowly.

When undertaking new business development activities, such as identifying targets of opportunity, most people find that they are most effective in calling on clones of their existing desirable clients. For example, I'm most comfortable working closely with intelligent and aggressive young professionals who know what they want from a consultant and who consequently use my time and talent effectively. These young pros are interested in getting things done, and will hold their consultants accountable for marketing in at least one or two major areas. I'm comfortable in handling and responding to their rapid-fire questions and "prove it to me" attitude. I enjoy working with them because I'm confident that they will respond to innovative procedures and will work to produce the desired results, as opposed to listening politely and then going back to conduct business as usual.

Working from within your comfort zone means calling on those prospects and suspects with whom you already have some type of familiarity and affinity.

These are people you are likely to feel comfortable calling on, because you can speak their business language and have an insider's understanding of their industry. Consequently, your anxiety should remain at an acceptable level.

This chapter has described the client-centered marketing approach and the client-centered marketing system. In so doing, it has provided a macro classification system for existing clients. We are now ready to proceed to Chapter 2, where we will take an in-depth micro look at your existing clients.

2

Classifying and Targeting Your Existing Clients

Now that we have a broad, macro-level perspective of the client-centered marketing and service approach, it is time to take a micro look at your existing clients and to classify them according to their target categories.

I will begin by showing you how to develop a profile of existing clients. It provides you with a method you will never outgrow regardless of the nature and size of your practice. Using this profile, you can classify each client according to its potential for opportunity as well as for problems.

After each client has been classified, you will have a maxtrix of current clients that you can use to leverage your time. Clients are identified in a way that allows you to identify priorities in making your business decisions for the upcoming period.

The logic involved in developing a profile of one's current clients has been tried successfully and put into practice by hundreds of my clients over the years. Experience has shown that service professionals can experience rapid and profitable growth from using the information contained in this chapter. The classification system will be referred to throughout the subsequent chapters of this book.

To simplify the discussion, I have developed several exhibits which I will refer to as we proceed.

DEVELOPING A PROFILE OF YOUR EXISTING CLIENTS

The first step in client-target classification is to develop a profile of existing clients. The profile is designed to include the three broad classes of clients identified in Chapter 1, and then further divide them into subclasses. This simple analysis yields significant dividends.

ASSEMBLE AND PROCESS INFORMATION ABOUT YOUR CLIENT BASE

Exhibit 2-1, the "Client Performance and Potential Profile," has been prepared to assist you in acquiring the information you will need to develop and process your profile. A spreadsheet program can be used to enter and compute the required information.

Before you begin preparing the worksheet, rank your current clients in terms of the largest fee to the smallest fee generated during the most recent 12 months. Then perform the following steps.

1. List clients you will continue to serve during the next 12 months.

2. List clients you are now serving for the first time and estimate the fees to be generated during the next 12 months. Enter this amount as (+) in column 4.

Exhibit 2-1. Client Performance and Potential Profile

(1) Client Name	(2) Most Recent 12-Month Fees	(3) % of Total Fee	(4) Estimated Net (+) (−) Fees Next Period	(5) (a) SIC	(b) ZIP
	Total $ xxxx	100%	Total Net (+) (−) $ xxxxx		

Worksheet

(6) Quality of Relationship (1–5)	(7) Referral Source	(8) Potential for Providing Additional Service High, "H"; Medium, "M"; Low, "L"		(9) Client Classification	(10) Target Category
		Short-Term	Long-Term		

3. List clients you will serve for the first time in the next 12 months and estimate the fees to be generated during this period. Enter this amount as (+) in column 4.

4. List the names of any clients you served in the past 12 months but will lose in the next period, and enter the total fees earned in columns 2 and 4. Show the fee as (−) in column 4.

5. For each client listed in steps 1–4, enter the latest 12-month fee, estimated net fees (+ or −) for the next period, and four-digit SIC.

6. Compute the total fees represented by the clients, and the percentage of the total fee represented by each client.

7. Print out the worksheet with columns 1–5 completed.

8. For each listed client, estimate the quality of primary client–firm relationship on a scale of 1 to 5, with 1 being totally unsatisfactory and 5 being excellent.

9. Place "Y" in column 7 if the client makes referrals in your behalf.

10. Estimate the potential for providing additional services to each client in column 8. Use an "H" for high, "M" for medium, and "L" for low to represent this potential. *Short-term* refers to the next 12 months; *long-term* is beyond 12 months.

11. Classify each client in terms of its overall potential. Use Exhibit 2-2, "Criteria for

Classifying Your Existing Clients," and assign the proper letter class for each client in column 9.

12. Use Exhibit 2-3, "Current Target Categories," page 36, to assign each client to the appropriate target category, and enter this in column 10.

Appendix B contains additional material to assist you in preparing and using this simple and powerful profile.

Exhibit 2-2. Criteria for classifying your existing clients.

Desirable Clients

1. *Mega Clients*: Clients of such fee magnitude that you can't afford to lose the relationship.

2. *Key Clients*: Clients that make referrals to others in your behalf, have strong potential for fee growth, are receptive to additional constructive service ideas, and frequently provide you with excellent opportunities to develop your skills and information base.

3. *"A" Clients*: Clients you hope will develop into Key clients. They willingly pay their fees, are generally receptive to additional service discussions, and may be educated into making referrals at a later date.

4. *"B" Clients*: These clients are your bread and butter clients. They pay their bills, don't give you too much grief, but

---

31

Exhibit 2-2. Continued.

do not represent potential for good fee growth.

Unknown at This Time

1. Clients you are now serving for the first time.

2. Newly acquired clients you are yet to begin serving.

Undesirable

1. *"C" Clients*: These clients seek discounts, and additional free services, and are frequently slow in paying your invoices.

2. *"D" Clients*: These are the clients you wish you had never accepted in the first place. They often operate on the margin of ethical performance, and are not averse to pressuring you to compromise your personal and professional standards.

Now that clients are classified as Mega, Key, A, B, Unknown, C, or D, you have in your possession a worksheet for entering data into any spreadsheet software program that can produce the data outputs for the classification system.

Number and dollar value for each *group* of clients should be computed to yield strategic insights into the nature and scope of your current client base. Additionally, clients should be listed individually within each class by amount of fee, from lowest to highest. This listing provides you with a sharper profile of your current practice that is useful in establishing goals and priorities as you classify your clients into appropriate target categories.

MAJOR EXISTING CLIENT GOALS

Now that you have your clients classified, it is important to establish procedures that allow you to modify and review your client profile as needed. This will assist you in making business decisions and charting the course of firm policy. The next step is to identify goals for existing clients.

General Goals

Through the administration of your client-centered marketing program, your general goals will be to:

- Maintain a current inventory of existing clients classified by their current fees and their potential for providing you with:

  Additional revenue:

  Immediately

  Short-term (within 12 months)

  Long-term

Additional referrals

Financial problems

Professional difficulties

- Identify and manage known and suspected revenue losses/shortfalls during the next period.

Desirable Client Goals

In the development of your client-centered marketing strategies, the goals you will seek to achieve with desirable clients include the following.

- Deliver value-perceived services in a timely, efficient, mutually beneficial manner.

- Build and retain client-centered, value-added relationships with key client executives in Mega, Key, and "A" client organizations.

- Provide additional assignments by sensing the needs of clients and bringing them to the attention of the decision maker(s).

- Obtain leads, introductions and "vouch-for" testimonials from all desirable clients.

- Quickly identify early warnings of client problems and dissatisfaction, and responsively undertake diagnostic and corrective actions to strengthen and retain primary client-firm relationships with desirable clients.

- Capitalize on engagements with desirable clients.

- Determine and capitalize on sources of desirable clients.

- Empower all who are involved in and impacted on by the delivery and implementation of each service solution.

Undesirable Client Goals

The goals you will seek to achieve in regard to your undesirable clients are the following.

- Determine the correctable causes of current "C" clients and seek to upgrade them to at least "B" status.

- Determine correctable causes of current "D" clients and attempt to upgrade them at least to a "B" status, or consider replacing them if warranted.

- Determine the causes of current undesirable clients, and seek to remove them.

ASSIGNING CLASSIFIED CLIENTS INTO CURRENT TARGET CATEGORIES

After your clients have been categorized by class, you can assign each to a *current target category* within each category. Exhibit 2-3 provides the criteria used to assign each client a target category.

Exhibit 2-3. Current target categories.

Targets of Opportunity

1. Existing Mega, Key, and "A" clients with:

    needs for additional services

    a budget to pay for their fulfillment

    a willingness to discuss their needs
    with you

2. Existing prospective clients

Targets of Attention

1. Desirable clients with potential for up-
    grading of client class:

    "A" clients who can become Key clients
    by making referrals

    "B" clients with potential for upgrading

2. Unknown clients who need to be clas-
    sified

3. Undesirable "C" clients that can be up-
    graded by reducing discounts or speeding
    up payment of invoices

4. Potential clients in your area you need to
    contact

Targets of Concern

1. Desirable clients with warning signals:

    Known/suspected to be dissatisfied with
    your service

    Targeted by other firms

> Key clients no longer making referrals
>
> No longer receptive to discussing additional services
>
> Engagements no longer profitable
>
> May be merger candidates
>
> 2. Undesirable clients with warning signals:
>
> "C" clients from whom discounts or receivables are growing
>
> "D" clients who are becoming more troublesome or risky

As an ongoing part of your client profile, you should maintain a current inventory of existing clients classified according to their *current target categories* within each class of client. This should be done on a periodic basis. The target can be further refined in terms of attention priority: immediate, short-term (within the next 12 months), and long-term (beyond 12 months).

Once target categories have been assigned, you possess an intensive analysis of your client base that will enable you to leverage your time in making sound, pragmatic business decisions. This client profile, which will be referred to in later chapters of the book, forms the foundation necessary for putting the skills of client-centered marketing to use.

3

Developing Value-Added Relationships

A *value-added relationship* differs from most of the professional relationships that a service provider maintains. A professional relationship can be defined as one in which the service provider is responsive to the terms spelled out in the initial letter of agreement, referred to as an *engagement letter*. A value-added relationship goes beyond this; it evolves to a point where the service provider may be accepted as a "partner" in the business operations of the client organization.

Valued-added relationships are developed with only a small handful of clients at any one time. They are built with clients you have targeted for special treatment in order to ensure retention of the primary client–firm relationship or to provide a vehicle for developing additional revenue, referrals, and related business goals.

GOALS OF RELATIONSHIP DEVELOPMENT

In the development and maintenance of special client–firm relationships, your goals will be to do the following:

1. To create *level* primary client–firm relationships. (The characteristics of a *level* relationship are described later in this chapter.)
2. To create and nurture special relationships with leverage players in the client's organization, and with significant individ-

uals who have external influence on client personnel.

3. To shift from occasional service provider to a continuing source of resources and advice by creating board-level perceptions and relationships.

4. To transform your mind-set, and the client's view of you, from that of consultant-server to one of a trusted mentor who is perceived as a specialized resource provider and quality assurance controller working in the client's best interest.

5. To consciously plan for and create enhanced relationships that result in:

   • increased levels of trust in your judgment, commitment, and continuity.

   • increased receptivity to recommendations made by you regarding additional services you can and should provide.

   • increased comfort and affinity with you and your assigned staff.

This process involves a sequence of steps and contacts, each of which has as its purpose a deepening and expansion of existing and desired relationships. Because this is an expensive undertaking, you need to make a well-informed decision before beginning the costly development process.

One of the major benefits you will obtain through the establishment of value-added relationships is the retention of your primary client—

firm relationships. Business executives come and go, and occasionally you will lose points of contact. But if you have established the proper relationships throughout the client's organization, you will still have points of access to the organization.

As an example, I work with a number of national and international service firms. My primary client–firm relationships are with the head office directors of marketing, and my secondary and supporting relationships are with the individuals responsible for their firm's Continuing Professional Education (CPE). I ask for copies of their directories so I can establish relationships and, I hope, selling and service points of contact with key partners in charge of local offices. This way, if an executive leaves a client organization, my primary client–firm relationship remains intact, and I remain in good shape.

To illustrate how this process works, one of the best multiple relationship situations I have developed is with an international accounting firm with offices in close to 100 cities in North America. Shortly after I was hired, I learned that the director of marketing would be leaving soon. I had worked with his chief deputy, who I had reason to believe would soon be promoted to director of marketing. He was a younger fellow eager to make his mark, and he wanted to install a workable marketing plan as quickly as possible. My reading of his personality was that he would cut me loose shortly after I identified those opportunities within the firm where the marketing department could win early, often, and visibly.

In the three weeks prior to the departure of the existing marketing director, I arranged to meet with the CPE director, who was responsible for supporting the firm's new marketing functions. I gave him a number of freebies in the form of ideas, informal instruction, workbook sections, and information about approaches he could include in his curriculum. My *value-added factor* was that I was ready and able to share ideas that assisted him in the development of his curriculum—ideas that I knew had already been accepted within the marketing department. This made it much easier for him to instruct partners and managers for whom marketing was a new and somewhat intimidating responsibility.

Because of this secondary "support" relationship, I was soon conducting executive briefing sessions for members of the Management Committee, and the departure of the director of marketing had little impact on my standing with the firm. The Management Committee was composed of key local office partners as well as upper management officials. These briefings led to my being hired to provide in-office marketing seminars at 25 regional offices nationwide.

TRADITIONAL VERSUS NONTRADITIONAL MARKETING

Clients don't really purchase services from service providers; they purchase the expectations of receiving a better future. A professional is hired because he or she is specially trained and experienced in a way that will help client executives identify solutions to problems and perform tasks that will improve the economic performance and efficiency of their organization.

Traditionally, service professionals have assumed that growth is a natural by-product of producing good technical services and meeting the demands of the marketplace. This is a passive approach, wherein professionals rely on clients to contact them in regard to a specific need. In today's competitive world, this passivity places severe limitations on the potential for growth.

Another traditional approach is the hard sell, wherein a heavy emphasis is placed on cultivating a reputation and becoming well known within a particular market. The working assumption here is that reputation breeds new business, which may prove true in the short run but does not provide a long-term strategy for ongoing client-based marketing development. The major weakness of the hard sell is that it is not need-driven, but is geared toward selling those services the professional happens to be good at or can easily provide.

A client-centered approach differs from the traditional methods in that it is *need-driven*. Rather than remaining passive and waiting for the client to identify a specific need, the client-centered service provider tries to examine the needs of the client by mentally sitting on the client's side of the desk to view the client's needs and objectives.

Instead of trying to sell a traditional service, or a package of services, the client-centered professional tailors services to meet client needs in innovative ways. One of those methods is through communication that leads to the establishment of valued-added relationships.

For example, one of my clients has a *Real Estate Factors Alert*, which is prepared for a select group of bank lending officers. Written in a concise newsletter format, the *Alert* gives readers insider information of a strictly local nature that is unavailable through traditional sources. This newsletter not only enhances communication by creating numerous topics for discussion, but also gives the client a tangible product that automatically increases his pool of available information.

Another consulting firm has established a modem and telephone line connection with a client for whom it provides specialized analytical services. The client is delighted by the rapid, real-time response and by the availability of the information.

In my practice, I also attempt to develop value-added relationships by providing my best clients with my private, unlisted telephone number. I stress the fact that this number is not available to others, but only to my most important clients. I also make it a point to follow up on my clients, and to celebrate their victories. Recently, I called one of my newer public relations firm clients, who was struggling with his receivables. I inquired about various aspects of his business, and then mentioned the names of a couple of accountants who had expertise in his area of concern. His response was warm, and he mentioned several times that he was pleased that I cared enough to call him and share my ideas with him. It turned out that he did employ the services of one of the accountants to whom I had referred him, and his problem was ironed out within a matter of weeks. This gave me the opportunity to place a follow-up call and congratulate him on his success. I also strengthened my relationship with a non-client referral source.

Perhaps this is just sound business practice, but over the years I have found that value-added service has brought revenue, referrals, and new clients to my practice.

LEVEL VERSUS VERTICAL RELATIONSHIPS

Once the engagement has been sold, the nature of the relationship and the way in which you deliver your services will be essential for the continuity of service opportunities. Business development is relationship development, and the service professional is always better off if she can develop *level* relationships rather than vertical relationships with the key people in the client's organization.

A *level relationship* occurs when both the professional providing the service and the client receiving the service view one another as team members of equal importance working toward the satisfaction of the client's needs or the solution of the client's problems. In this situation neither the client nor the professional assumes a superior position over the other.

A *vertical relationship* is characterized by an imbalance in authority, status, or importance. In this situation one party assumes authority over the other party.

The disadvantages of a vertical relationship are

1. It is difficult for a professional to successfully complete an engagement when the client assumes a superior attitude. A dominant attitude on the part of the client makes it more difficult to sense, serve, and satisfy the needs of that client.

2. If the professional assumes a dominant attitude, the client may hesitate to ask questions, may not develop an understanding of recommendations, and finally, may hesitate to implement the professional's recommendations.

3. A dominant attitude by either party decreases the potential for meaningful communication and increases the potential for conflict.

The advantages of a level relationship are

1. The potential for meaningful communication and cooperation is increased.

2. The potential for conflict is lessened.

3.   The potential for achieving a win-win relationship, in which both the client and the professional feel good about the outcome of the engagement, is increased.

Let's close this section by looking at two contrasting examples of level and vertical relationships.

A public relations firm client provided Issues Management services for a large association. Its initial point of contact was with the Executive Director, but its daily working contacts were vertical in nature since it reported to the in-house communications professional, who was very protective of her turf, and who did everything in her power to keep the client service team from having significant contact with the association's key decision makers. As a result, the service provider did not risk climbing over her front line of defense with each new proposal, and their relationship was on a project-by-project basis.

In contrast, a consulting friend of mine established level relationships with a large client by serving as a facilitator for her client's Executive Committee meetings. She worked her way into the inner sanctum and is regarded as a team player by the committee members. She is always present when new and important problems surface, and consequently she does not have to climb the corporate totem pole to discuss service opportunities. New business floats her way as a natural by-product of the level relationships she has cultivated.

THE ANATOMY OF CLIENT—FIRM RELATIONSHIPS

A relationship involves two or more consenting people who invest their time and other things of value for the purpose of meeting recognized needs in ways that meet their expectations and offset their costs and risks. Clients want to have their needs met in a way that not only fulfills their expectations, but more than offsets the costs they perceive as being involved in the relationship. In the initial engagement, the service professional should pay special attention to ensure that the client perceives the benefits that accrue from the investment, and that the client's expectations are being fully considered.

In addition to money, the things of value that clients invest frequently include their time, the time of their staff, and the information that must be made available to the members of the engagement team. Many clients are reluctant to "open the corporate kimono," and divulge proprietary information about their organization until they have developed a high level of trust in the service provider.

The client's expectations about the way in which he and his people will be treated by the service professional(s) who are meeting his need(s) include politeness, responsiveness, and a professional manner during the conduct of the engagement. In addition, some clients expect a degree of "handholding" at various stages of the process, or extra services that go beyond ordinary practice. There may also be other unexpressed expectations, such as not smoking on company premises and not talking with people other than those immediately concerned with the engagement. These expectations should be taken as seriously as traditional job performance criteria because they often serve as "go/ no-go" criteria for continuing or terminating the relationship.

Several examples will illustrate the importance of being sensitive to client expectations.

In one new client situation in which I was to convene a strategic planning session, I was told by the chief executive: "Let the chips fall where they may. We are big boys and we can handle the truth when it needs to be said." That caused my antenna to rise a bit. In probing what the client meant by letting the chips fall, I soon realized that it was okay for his people to be exposed, but that he did not want anyone to make him look bad in front of the troops or his wife, who was a major player in the firm. In conducting the planning session my strategy was to suggest that truth-telling is fine in small doses and to solicit non–ego-threatening evaluations for areas in need of improvement. Had I not probed for the inner meaning of my client's words, and therefore permitted the total candor he had claimed to want, I would have been shut out of the relationship much sooner than either of us desired.

Another common example is serving a client who expects that throwaway questions such as "How can I really improve my profit on line item X?" will be answered off the cuff and not billed for. I cover how to deal with scope changes in another part of the book, but it is important to maintain control over unreasonable client expectations, and to prevent throwaway questions from becoming expensive-to-deliver freebies.

In new client situations where I know, or suspect, that I am the replacement for another firm, I try to elicit client expectations at the start of the engagement. I do so by asking the client about her experience in dealing with my type of firm, and ask her to answer the question, "How will you and I both know when I'm doing a good job for you?" This gives her an opportunity to describe goals and expectations, and it provides me with an opportunity to differentiate between long-range objectives and immediate job requirements. For example, one client answered my question by saying that we would both know I was doing a good job, "When every one of my partners is bringing in the equivalent of his total compensation in new clients." I replied by saying, "That is a terrific future goal—after we complete the sales training program." Then I turned his attention to the first step in the process, namely, the implementation of the training program. This future goal was immediately entered into a client service plan, which will be discussed in Chapter 6.

DEVELOPING VALUE-ADDED RELATIONSHIPS

How are level value-added relationships developed and maintained? The building of a value-added relationship is a four-step process that includes (1) building the esteem of the client, (2) solidifying the professional relationship, (3) building a personal relationship, and (4) developing an ongoing exchange relationship. Each of these four steps will be discussed in turn.

Building the Esteem of a Client

A sound engagement-service relationship is initially based on meeting the terms of service that have been spelled out in the engagement letter. The first essential step in going beyond this professional relationship to a value-added relationship is to build the esteem of key client personnel.

Esteem building is initially done in need-related, job-specific conversations with client executives. The purpose is to make the other person feel good about himself and feel comfortable with you. This should not be mere flattery, but should legitimately acknowledge the individual's excellence in some area that is of importance of him.

Esteem is built by success, recognition, acceptance, and belief in what one is doing. It is threatened by criticism, reprimands, rejection, and failure to provide adequate feedback. Therefore, the goals are to provide positive feedback when it is warranted and to maintain positive, open channels of communication whenever problems arise.

Exhibit 3-1 lists several esteem-building questions you can work into conversations with your

Exhibit 3-1. Esteem-building questions you can ask a client.

> How did you remain profitable and succeed while the overall industry was in a downward trend?
>
> What are your predictions on market trends for the next year?
>
> How do you find the time and energy to be involved/ manage a successful business and still _____?
>
> What is your secret in keeping your key people?
>
> It appears that you are outpacing your competition in _____. What are you doing that is working so well?
>
> How have you continually increased sales by such a large percentage?
>
> How have you managed to remain such an innovative force in your industry?
>
> What do you attribute your success to?
>
> I understand that _____ occurred. How were you able to make that happen in spite of present conditions?
>
> What do you see happening in _____ [a critical success area in the industry]?
>
> How did you happen to develop an expertise in _____?
>
> What trends do you see emerging in _____?

desirable clients. Exhibit 3-2 provides numerous actions you can undertake to help build the esteem of key individuals. Becoming aware of opportunities to build client esteem and then acting on those opportunities help to level the relationship and lay the foundation for a value-added relationship.

Exhibit 3-2. Esteem-building actions.

Answer/return the client's phone calls promptly.

Send the client articles of interest.

Buy a book for the client that flatters him.

Contribute to the client's charities, and thank her for making you aware of the opportunity to do so.

Invite the client to participate in a firm function.

Invite the client to a social event.

Compliment the client on a particular action he took that was of help to you.

Ask the client to speak to your professional staff.

Introduce the client to other influentials.

Take the client to dinner in appreciation of _____.

Speak well of the client among the people she respects.

Send a letter to congratulate the client on an accomplishment.

Solidifying the Professional Relationship

This is done by being responsive to client needs throughout the course of the engagement, and by pointing out benefits and showing how you have exceeded expectations to make positive results visible to the client.

As you perform these job-related functions, you will want to increase your client-centered understanding of the client. This means that you will begin to think and relate beyond the boundaries of the traditional current project-oriented relationship. The goal is to elevate the focus of your attention to include an awareness and understanding of the subjects and problems discussed by the client at the boardroom level. As you begin to acquire this understanding, you will gradually shift away from engagement-specific communications to a broader range of need-benefit communications. Exhibit 3-3 lists examples of the type of actions you can take to solidify the professional relationship.

Exhibit 3-3. Actions to solidify the professional relationship.

Attend trade association meetings with the client.

Take the client to lunch and discuss business.

Deliver quality service; deliver more than what is expected.

Exhibit 3-3. Continued.

> Learn as much as you can about the client's business and industry.
>
> Share "tips" and other information with the client.
>
> Join and be active in the client's industry and trade associations.
>
> Provide publications of direct interest and benefit to the client.
>
> Discuss additional services as they relate to uncertainties and critical success factors.
>
> Sustain contacts year round.
>
> Conduct face-to-face post engagement "satisfaction" meetings.

Building a Personal Relationship

A personal relationship often evolves quite naturally from continued client contacts. The earlier esteem-building actions and the growth of your client-centered understanding help in this process. The key is to do this in a natural, relaxed manner. You want to communicate to clients that you care about them as people outside the office. The best ways to do this are to participate in activities of mutual interest and to recognize things that are of importance to the client.

For some, the next step may come prior to this one, but the important point is that value-added relationships evolve over time and must be planned for. This chapter provides you with the knowledge necessary to begin targeting appropriate clients and to take the steps that lead to this evolutionary process. Exhibit 3-4 identifies actions and strategies you can employ to help build personal relationships with targeted clients.

Exhibit 3-4. Actions to build personal relationships.

Entertain the client as appropriate.

Recognize personal events such as birthdays and anniversaries.

Send seasonal greetings.

Participate in activities of mutual interest and extend invitations when appropriate.

Be honest. Don't evade or hide from problems or errors. Admit it when help is needed, and involve other talented people.

Make references to yourself and your personal life so that the client sees you as an individual.

Develop an Ongoing Exchange Relationship

An exchange relationship occurs when a service professional provides his resources to meet a client need and the client provides her resources to meet the service professional's needs. Many people refer to this as "selling," but in reality it is a problem-solving process whereby the client agrees to pay the professional for solving a problem.

To develop an exchange relationship, the mindset on the part of the service professional must include a willingness to answer this question: In what ways can I serve as a conduit to the resources I have available in order to help this client do better at what she is in business to do? The goal is to shift from being viewed as service provider to being seen as a boardroom advisor and part-time partner in planning mutually profitable ventures. This requires a level relationship, whereby you are mentally sitting on the client's side of the desk, looking at his terrain through interested and knowledgeable eyes. The client, in turn, sees you as a conduit to valued resources and as a quality control contact capable of ensuring high-quality service.

In my own service practice I regularly attend partner meetings for my targeted high-potential-service firm clients. In those meetings I use the term "we," and I feel comfortable doing so because the client knows that I am dedicated to the same goals and objectives and that my own self-interest is never allowed to intrude on what is in the client's best interest. Of course, I am always careful not to cave in on matters of professional principle and practice.

As an example, one specific exchange relationship I have developed is with a consulting engineering firm. This is a local firm, so it is easy for me to attend the weekly management meeting. I attend the meeting every week that I'm in town, but I seldom bill the client for my input because the client allows me to use its laser printer and will sometimes write a line of computer code for me. I make frequent "I was thinking about you" telephone calls to let my contacts know they are important to me. I also don't hesitate to ask them for referrals or to bounce new business ideas off them.

THE BENEFITS OF VALUE-ADDED RELATIONSHIPS

If you strive to develop level relationships, and take the four steps required to develop value-added relationships with targeted clients, numerous benefits will accrue. But you should keep in mind that this is a lengthy process. You will, of course, strive to deliver quality service to all of your clients, but value-added relationships are only for those 10 or 15 percent of your clients who deserve the very best.

The benefits you will receive from going the extra mile include an assurance of client retention and protection from price competition. Highly satisfied clients are not going to be receptive to discounts offered by another service provider when they know they have a valued resource in the services that you provide. Another benefit is that you can work within your comfort zone on all engagements because revenue enhancement will be a by-product of the relationship rather than the motivating force behind it.

In the next chapter I'll show you how to begin building some client-centered marketing ideas and tools into your ongoing engagement procedures.

4

Building Marketing into the Engagement Process

In the preceding chapters, I have described what client-centering marketing is, how it differs from traditional marketing approaches, and how a client-centered approach to job performance can be used to build special types of value-added, level relationships.

In this chapter we will turn our attention to the development of engagement procedures with existing Mega, Key, and "A" clients that are designed to create profitable new sources of revenue with those clients. As a by-product, these business practices will also serve to protect revenue currently being derived from desirable clients that may be targeted by other firms.

BUILDING A SERVICE PROMOTION SYSTEM FOR EXISTING CLIENTS

In the preparation of a service promotion system for existing clients, your goal is to use the knowledge at your disposal to maximize the potential for deriving revenue from the business relationships you have already established. Exhibit 4-1 shows the elements of a service promotion system for existing clients. Several of the elements that compose the service promotion system for existing clients will be discussed.

Data Collection Procedures

The relevant procedures include the following.

Exhibit 4-1. Service promotion system for existing clients.

- Data collection procedures
  - Discussion initiation and review
  - Need-specific service targets
- New business discussion package
  - Question sheet
  - Testimonials
  - PAR reports
  - Sample final reports and other "deliverables"
  - Other firm and promotional materials
- Proposals
- Client-centered analysis

Discussion Initiation and Review

It is important to ensure that every business engagement you have with desirable clients with the potential for growth (1) be focused on points that yield actionable information, and (2) provide you with the ability to talk with knowledgeable and influential client personnel. It is also imperative that the information obtained from such engagements not be confined to your personal files or entrusted to memory. A desirable client discussion review form that catalogues the information derived should be maintained after each business contact. This does not have to be an elaborate document. A simple notation of what was covered, with whom, when, where, and with what results, in addition to any promised or planned next steps, is sufficient.

Need-Specific Service Targets

The data collected and kept on file should be analyzed to help you target client needs. New business discussions will be based on the needs identified as a result of data analysis. The Client Alert Report, discussed in Chapter 5, is an excellent example of the type of document used for this purpose.

New Business Discussion Package

The package is composed of five elements, each of which is discussed below.

The Question Sheet

The preparation of a question sheet will help guide you through the discussion of your client's potential new business situation. Naturally, the questions will differ for each discussion since they need to be tailored to meet the considerations of the service being offered. An example of a question sheet of this type is contained in Exhibit 4-2. I use this in determining the readiness of a professional firm to develop and install a client-centered marketing function in its organization.

Exhibit 4-2. Question sheet to determine a firm's readiness to establish a marketing function.

1. Do you have a recognized marketing champion in-house who is willing and capable of heading the function?

2. Do you have a clearly developed and communicated mission statement or vision for the firm or office?

3. To what extent is marketing responsibility assigned, articulated, understood, and accepted?

4. To what extent is marketing built into your performance and reward systems?

5. What percentage of total gross fees has been invested in marketing over the past three years?

6. What are the current and desired nature and scope of the practice in each functional specialty?

7. How often do partners and others meet to discuss marketing?

8. To what extent is a keep-off-my-turf attitude and behavior alive and well in the firm?

Testimonial Letters

Because you are expanding the range of services you are offering your client, statements of praise and commendation from satisfied clients already using the service under question can demonstrate the viability of this service and underscore the potential gains to be derived from the service. These statements should be kept on file as a permanent part of your promotion system.

PAR Reports

These are problem-approach-results write-ups from previous engagements. They should be used to demonstrate how similar problems have been met through the employment of your service in the targeted area. As is true with testimonials, PAR reports should be included as a standard part of your promotion system. They form an important part of your niche data base and help make your client aware of the benefits and solutions that can be obtained from the employment of your service. An example of a PAR report is contained in Exhibit 4-3.

Sample Final Reports

You should also maintain a file of sample final reports that satisfied clients have given you permission to use. These can be used to show how you tailor your materials to satisfy client needs and enhance the client's image. Be certain to block out any confidential client information!

Other Firm and Promotional Materials

Relevant firm promotional material and articles relating to your service should also be kept on file and incorporated into the new business package.

Exhibit 4-3. A problem-approach-results (PAR) report.

INDUSTRY: Local Government
OFFICE: Milwaukee

PROBLEM SITUATION

A class action suit had been filed against a city for releasing untreated sewage into public waters. The class action was for loss of business and punitive damages. Actual damages claimed were $1 billion from over 100 businesses. The client asked us to provide litigation support to substantiate damage losses.

ABC CO. SOLUTION

ABC would provide the professional and technical assistance needed to substantiate the business losses.

RESULTS EXPERIENCED BY CLIENT

The city provided a draft of the documentation request written by in-house legal counsel. This document was modified by ABC because of its experience in the business environment. As a result of the documentation request, we were informed that all of the suits were dropped except one, and it was not being pursued at this time.

Proposals

Previous proposals that document the way you delivered solutions to meet the need under consideration are invariably helpful in the preparation of new proposals. Therefore, they should be kept on file or in template form on your computer. A few minor changes to a previous proposal, including the addition of new client-centered data, are often all that is required.

DATA COLLECTION AND SERVICE DELIVERY

An operational service delivery system is an indispensable tool for facilitating data collection and the development of a resource bank for your service promotion system. At the end of each client engagement, a system should be in place to maintain a permanent record of the information derived from the work that has been done and to document the various stages of service delivery. Exhibit 4-4 shows the elements of a tried and true system that was used at an international consulting firm I once worked for. The various elements of the service delivery system are examined in the pages that follow.

Client-specific Documents

The Engagement Letter

This letter should contain the vital information describing the specifics of the engagement.

Special attention should be given to emphasizing the goal to be achieved and to the benefits derived by the client from employing the service. Appendix C is a complete guide to preparing a client-centered engagement letter.

Exhibit 4-4. A service delivery system.

Client-specific Documents

- Engagement letter
- Progress reports
- Final report/other deliverables
- Client satisfaction review

Engagement Administration

- Work Plan
- Budget
- Activity schedules
- Quality control procedures
- Invoice preparation

Engagement Wrap-Up

- PAR produced
- Press release, if significant client
- Recommendations for additional service
- Engagement distillation
- Inputs to standard practice manuals

Exhibit 4-4. Continued.

- Purchase detail: trigger for the purchase, title(s) for best contact
- Standard patterns, fee ranges, appropriate and expected jargon, buzz words
- Individual responsibilities

Progress Reports

In order to emphasize the client-centered nature of your services, progress reports should be customized in a way that exhibits your approach to specific client needs. It is best to limit boilerplate language to only the recurring aspects of the engagement.

Final Report and Other Deliverables

The final report must be customized to focus on client needs and benefits. It should justify the costs of the service to the client and once again emphasize the benefits derived. The report should be presented in a way that clearly demonstrates that the benefits exceed the costs. Delivery of the final report should always be done in person at a meeting scheduled in advance. This meeting can be used to discuss additional services.

Client Satisfaction Review

This stage is often overlooked, with many service professionals simply assuming that their job is complete with the delivery of the final report. The client satisfaction review not only ensures that client needs have been met, but also underscores the fact that you are conscious of client needs and expectations.

Engagement Administration

The Work Plan

A work plan, prepared in advance, enables you to estimate what resources will be required to provide the service under discussion and allows you to estimate a fee during the proposal phase of the process.

Budget

Time and dollar budgets should be estimated for each task, and the costs associated with those tasks. This allows you to estimate the total cost of the engagement.

Activity Schedules

List the daily tasks that must be undertaken at all levels to provide the service. This delineates specific firm responsibilities and allows you to tailor your resources to meet specific client needs.

Quality Control Procedures

Such procedures are normally standardized within your firm. However, modifications should be made within the process whenever it is necessary to meet special goals or client needs.

Engagement Wrap-Up

PAR Write-Up

The PAR should be reviewed with both the engagement team and the client, and should be completed only after the client satisfaction review has been conducted. When shared with the client, the PAR provides you with an excellent opportunity to elicit testimonials that can be incorporated into your service promotion package. It also provides an opportunity to explore additional needs and client problems.

Press Release and Relevant Publicity

For significant engagements, it is helpful to remember that all clients appreciate, and are impressed by, any positive publicity that can be generated. In essence, positive publicity is free advertising. The potential for either a press release or the authorship of a joint article should be examined for all significant engagements. Be certain to obtain approval from your client.

Recommendations for Additional Services

You should use the knowledge you have obtained about your client to suggest recommendations for additional services you want the client to consider at this time. These recommendations should reflect both client needs and client benefits. Relevant elements of the service promotion system for existing clients should be initiated here.

Figure 4-5. End-of-Engagement Report.

	Engagement No.
Client	
Assignment	Staff _____
	_____
To	_____
Submitted by	
	Supervision
	In Charge

Exhibit 4-5. Continued.

FINANCIAL RESULTS

	PROPOSED	ACTUAL	VARIANCES
Labor			
Fees			
Expenses			
Total			

CLIENT FEEDBACK

● Positive _____
_____

● Negative _____
_____

APPROACH

● Successful Techniques _____

_____

_____

_____

● Unsuccessful Techniques _____

_____

_____

● Other Feedback for Bidding and Performing Similar Engagement _____

_____

_____

_____

75

Engagement Distillation

Use your client engagements to upgrade your firm's niche information base and to increase the overall capabilities, procedures, and information available to your firm. This frequently over-looked process can provide valuable information. Exhibit 4-5 shows an End-of-Engagement Report, which is a handy form to use.

By building the factors discussed in this chapter into your engagement system, you will be able to reap the benefits of a planned approach to marketing while conducting the ongoing aspects of your engagements. Congratulations! You are now well on the way to building a successful marketing and client service system that will pay dividends for you in the years ahead.

Individual Responsibilities

Exhibit 4-6 shows the individual responsibilities by level of engagement. You'll want to modify this for your use because it incorporates all the marketing ideas discussed in this and subsequent chapters.

Exhibit 4-6. Individual marketing responsibilities with respect to existing clients, grouped by responsibility level.

Engagement Staff Personnel

• Develop sound relationships at assigned levels within the client organization.

- Identify needs for additional services during the engagement, and submit client satisfaction action recommendation* to the next level of responsibility.

- Identify "up-and-comers" in the client organization and make their identity known to the next level of responsibility.

- Contribute to the development of Client Service and Retention Plans (see Chapter 6).

Engagement Management Personnel

- Develop sound relationships at assigned levels within the client organization.

- Develop relationships with up-and-comers.

- Pre-sell needs for additional services.

- Manage the development of Client Service and Retention Plans (see Chapter 6).

- Contribute to the development of client referrals by making results visible.

Partners

- Capitalize on needs identified by staff and pre-sold engagement manager.

- Assign responsibility for development of Client Service and Retention Plans and participate in development as appropriate.

- Develop client referrals from satisfied clients.

Exhibit 4-6. Continued.

- Widen and deepen relationships with desirable client executives.

- Undertake upgrading activities with designated clients.

- Determine sources of desirable new clients and capitalize on opportunities.

- Determine reasons for lost clients and take corrective action.

- Terminate relationships with D clients as appropriate.

*You may use Client Alert Reports (see Chapter 5).

5

Using the Client Alert System

Existing client engagements can be a significant source of additional service projects and revenue if you capitalize on the opportunity they represent. By keeping your eyes and ears open, you are in a prime position to identify client needs, which provide you with additional opportunities to assist the client profitably. All members of your client engagement team should be trained and encouraged to identify these needs and to report on them in a systematic manner. By establishing this commitment, you will have taken an important step in sensing, serving, and satisfying client needs in a mutually profitable manner.

The Client Alert System provides a simple framework that is designed to capitalize on information gleaned from engagements with existing clients and on information obtained through observation and conversations with others in the client organization. The system is designed to work well within the comfort zone of everyone involved in the engagement.

The first step required for putting the system into operation is the dissemination and collection of Client Alert Report (CAR) forms. An example of a blank client alert report is shown in Exhibit 5-1 (pp. 82–83). The upper portion of the form, which is need-specific, provides space to describe data gleaned from direct participation in the engagement process. The sources of these data can be business documents, conversations with personnel, or direct observation. The middle section of the document provides space for rumors and other information that may or may not be fact but deserve further investigation. The lower portion of the report provides space for recommending and monitoring future actions that are deemed appropriate.

A person working on a project with a client is in a position to obtain information and make observations about the business practices of that client. The upper portion of the form is designed to break need-specific information down into three basic units. They are (1) what you were doing when you discovered the need; (2) what the need is, where it is located, where its effects are evident, who is involved, what it is costing the client, and the benefit to the client when solved; and (3) what will be improved, reduced, saved, or answered.

An example of how the upper portion of the form could be completed (with segment numbers in brackets) would read as follows: [1] As a result of reviewing the accounting procedures at Company X, [2] I discovered that the manager of the marketing department liked to do PR, but he has inadequate control over his staff. Department heads quarrel frequently, and production costs for promotional materials often appear to be out of line. [3] An operational management audit should permit implementation of new organization and systems to improve overall performance and profitability.

Exhibit 5-1. Client Alert Report (blank).

Client: _____ SIC # _____ Engagement Partner: _____

Prepared by: _____ Date ___/___/___

Approved by: ___Supervisor/Manager___ Date ___/___/___

Known/Suspected Need: As a result of _____ (what you were doing when you personally discovered the need)

I discovered that _____ (state succinctly: what the need is, where it is located, where its effects are evident, who is

involved, what is it costing the client, the benefit to the client when solved—what will be improved, reduced,

saved, answered?

_____

_____

_____

_____ AND/OR _____

Mr., Mrs., Miss, Ms. _____ , _____ , _____
(circle one)   First and Last Name   Position

Told me/remarked that _____ (State succinctly:
                        (circle one)

what the need is, where it is located, where its effects are evident, who is involved, what is it costing the client,

the benefit to the client when solved—what will be improved, reduced, saved, answered?

_____

_____

_____

Recommended Next Steps:

What	Who	Due Date	Done	Result
1.				
2.				
3.				

Route to: Personnel File _____
Engagement Partner _____
Partner in
    Charge _____
Practice Development
    Coordinator _____

83

Exhibit 5-2. Sample Client Alert Report (Jayes Mfg.)

Client: _Jayes Manufacturing Co._ ————— SIC # ——————— Engagement Partner: ———————

Prepared by: _Senior_ ———————————————— Date ___6 / 11 /X1___

Approved by: _Partner_ ———————————————— Date ___6 / 14 /X1___

      Supervisor/Manager

Known/Suspected Need: As a result of ___confirming accounts receivable___

          (what you were doing when you personally discovered the need)

I discovered that ___all payments were not timely posted to customer's accounts by business office cashier. Company is___

       (state succinctly: what the need is; where it is located, where its effects are evident, who is

losing the use of these funds and incurring clerical time in answering customer complaints. Next steps: Discuss need

 involved, what is it costing the client, the benefit to the client when solved—what will be improved, reduced,

for cash management system with client. (Could be part of management letter)

 saved, answered?

——

——

——

———————————————————— AND/OR ————————————————————

(Mr.,) Mrs., Miss, Ms. _____ Jim Smith _____, _____ Sales Manager _____ (Told me)/remarked that _____ projected sales for _____
(circle one)   First and Last Name   Position   (circle one)   (State succinctly:

the next 6 months are lower by 30% than budgeted last year. Labor costs have not been reduced to compensate for lower

what the need is, where it is located, where its effects are evident, who is involved, what is it costing the client,

sales.

the benefit to the client when solved—what will be improved, reduced, saved, answered?

_____

_____

Recommended Next Steps:

What	Who	Due Date	Done	Result
1. Recommend market/productivity study	Spvr/Ptr	ASAP		
2. Discuss with client the need to reduce	"	"		
3. labor costs				

Route to: Personnel File _____
Engagement Partner _____
Partner in
Charge _____
Practice Development
Coordinator _____

85

Exhibit 5-3. Sample Client Alert Report (XYZ, Inc.).

Client: ___XYZ, Inc._____ SIC # _____ Engagement Partner: _____

Prepared by: ___MB_____ Date ___6 / 11 /X1

Approved by: ___MB_____ Date ___6 / 11 /X1
               Supervisor/Manager

Known/Suspected Need: As a result of ___a feasibility study by the MAS Dept._____
_____ (what you were doing when you personally discovered the need)

I discovered that ___an investment tax credit study on the hotel to be built in Midland would maximize tax savings.___
_____ (state succinctly: what the need is, where it is located, where its effects are evident, who is
Coordinate sales effort with tax department.
involved, what is it costing the client, the benefit to the client when solved—what will be improved, reduced,
_____

saved, answered?
_____

_____

_____

_____

_____AND/OR_____

_____

(**Mr.,**) Mrs., Miss, Ms. _____Bill Jones_____ _____CEO_____ , his executive
(circle one) First and Last Name Position

(**Told me**)/remarked that (State succinctly:
(circle one)

managers are paying too much tax now and don't have enough for savings as a result. Need to talk to client about
what the need is, where it is located, where its effects are evident, who is involved, what is it costing the client,
deferred compensation plan. Nominal costs in relation to retained managers and lack of turnover.
the benefit to the client when solved—what will be improved, reduced, saved, answered?

_____

_____

Recommended Next Steps:

What	Who	Due Date	Done	Result
1. Explain potential saving to client	MAS & Tax Ptr	ASAP		
2. Make formal proposal in letter		When step 1 completed		
3.				

Route to: Personnel File _____
Engagement Partner _____
Partner in
Charge _____
Practice Development
Coordinator _____

Similarly, the middle portion of the form can be broken down into three basic elements in order to report on information picked up as a result of conversations with client personnel. These three elements are (1) name and position of the person who conveyed the information; (2) what the need is, where it is located, where its effects are evident, who is involved, what it is costing the client, and the benefit to the client when solved; and (3) what will be improved, reduced, saved, or answered.

Again putting these elements to use, an example of how the middle portion of the form could be completed would read as follows: [1] Mrs. Effie Smith, the secretary to the vice president in charge of new accounts, told me [2] that there are constant discrepancies in billing rates and expense vouchers, and that the daily "audit" rarely balanced. She was overworked because she had to reconcile these discrepancies herself. [3] It seems that there is a profit improvement potential of at least 20 percent through a reorganization and implementation of voucher controls, standardization of billing rates, and an improved accounting system.

The form is designed so that a wide variety of information can be contained in these reports, and these examples are intended merely as illustrations. Thousands of variations are possible; two examples of complete CARs are shown in Exhibits 5-2 and 5-3.

The key point is that observations, conversations, and rumors should be explored to obtain information about client needs and business practices. Quite often, such information is dismissed by engagement personnel who are not sensitive to the potential value of a Client Alert System. One of the key purposes of the form is to sensitize personnel to the importance of collecting and analyzing this information.

MANAGING CLIENT ALERT REPORTS

Every Mega, Key, and A client should have CARs prepared for every engagement that is undertaken on their behalf. Managing the distribution and preparation of these reports requires seven steps to initiate implementation of the system.

1. The engagement manager distributes the CARs to each staff person working on an in-field status.

2. If training is required, the engagement manager reviews the purpose of the CAR at the time of distribution and explains how and when the form is to be submitted.

3. At the time of distribution, the engagement manager also suggests areas for specific attention or concern, when appropriate, and identifies specific dates for submission to the partner.

4. Prior to the submission date, the engagement manager will want to remind staff personnel that the CARs are due.

5. Upon receipt of the CARs from the in-field staff, the engagement manager will review

the reports for completeness and potential value. If necessary, CARs will be returned to field staff for further work and more complete information.

6. If the initial CAR is acceptable, the engagement manager will determine if he or she should handle the factors discussed in the report. If the answer is no, the engagement manager will try to enhance or improve on the information contained in the report, sending the original to the partner and making copies for the relevant files. If the answer is yes, the engagement manager will flesh out the outline of recommended steps for further action and prepare a budget that shows the client benefits to be obtained from the service solution. These recommendations are then submitted to the partner for approval or revision, and relevant copies are placed on file.

7. The partner receives the CAR and takes immediate action as appropriate. The submitter of the CAR is notified of the status of any pending action and future outcomes.

CAPITALIZING ON CLIENT ALERT REPORTS

The purpose of obtaining and managing Client Alert Reports is to gather information that can help you expand the amount of revenue you receive from existing clients. To maximize the value of this information, seven follow-up steps should be undertaken that allow you to capitalize on the leads contained in your Client Alert Reports.

1. Separate leads into short-term and long-term opportunities.

2. Organize short-term leads as follows: those *within* your area of expertise and comfort zone, and those *outside* your area of expertise. In the latter case, you must either enhance the quality of the information contained in your CAR, or pass it on to the person with the relevant expertise.

3. Organize long-term opportunities as in step 2.

4. Handle the need. In doing so, you should review any appropriate workpapers, review previous management letters, contact internal experts to obtain additional information, contact up-and-comers in the client organization for additional thoughts and inputs, and consider the applicability of the envisioned service to other clients.

5. Develop a constructive service plan that defines the benefits to the client. The service plan should spell out who will be responsible for what actions at what costs and what benefits. In short, the service plan should describe the staff time and fees required.

6. Arrange to meet with your client. Prior to this meeting you should include your findings in a management letter to the appro-

priate contact. At the time of the meeting, you should discuss the situation and recommend a constructive service plan, with the objective of obtaining a commitment to proceed from the client. After obtaining a signed engagement letter or contract, the assignment should be put on the schedule.

7. The progress of any open CAR files should be monitored on a periodic basis. All actions taken should be recorded, and recognition should be awarded to those responsible for any positive outcomes achieved.

I hope that by now you understand that using the CAR is very beneficial. To further illustrate this point, I'm including the results obtained by two service firms.

• A computer services consulting firm in the Midwest adopted the CAR tool for their practice. They called the report their "Red Card." They provided training in the use of the Card and built the distribution and use of the Card into the ongoing engagement and engagement closeout procedures. To ensure that the Card was prepared and distributed correctly, the Executive Committee approved a policy that stated, in effect: "No Card, no engagement closeout, no credit toward end-of-the-year bonus." After a period of grumbling and attempts to subvert the system, most executives supported it and found that a substantial amount of previously unrecognized additional business was secured from their "captive" clients.

- An international accounting firm that instituted the Client Alert System without providing the training and policy guidelines never captured the business that was available within their client base. Management was not up to the task of confronting the culture and making the rules stick. Incredibly, several executives did use the system, and they had a much higher degree of success than their colleagues in the firm who failed to do so. To this day the more successful executives continue to involve a large number of their lower-level staff personnel in the important task of internal new business development.

6

Developing Client Service Plans

The Client Service Plan is designed to serve as your proprietary marketing information tool with desirable clients. It contains client-centered information that will be useful to you in retention planning, providing additional services, and educating you about the client's business, organization, and industry.

The Client Service Plan, when coupled with previous and current Client Alert Reports, provides you with a corporate memory and information bank regarding the client. When put into practice, client service planning will provide you with another tool you'll never outgrow that will pay dividends for years.

Determining the needs of existing Mega, Key, and "A" clients is your first and most important revenue enhancement activity. It should be an organized activity, undertaken for clients with whom you have a recurring relationship.

In order to meet client needs and expectations successfully, it is necessary to have a clear understanding of client goals and the benefits the client expects to receive from the employment of your services. At the most fundamental level, client service planning provides a tool for organizing and motivating your engagement team to identify client needs and to act in a coordinated way to make the client aware of services you can provide to address those needs.

A Client Service Plan will also help provide a link between the client and your engagement team. New personnel are more easily assimilated into engagements, others in the firm are more easily brought into the additional services loop, and the quality of key client–firm relationships is charted to show current strengths and weaknesses.

BENEFITS OF CLIENT SERVICE PLANNING

The Client Service Plan described in this chapter formalizes an approach that has been used by experienced professionals and corporations of all sizes worldwide to better serve their clients. It improves your service to clients because it helps you to recognize client needs and to respond to those needs. My years of experience in advising professional service clients has shown that the successful implementation of client service planning will enhance your ability to:

- Obtain more knowledge about a client (based on inputs that take advantage of *all* engagement team members).

- Identify a road map of personal contacts in the client organization that need strengthening or are linked to specific service opportunities.

- Assess what is unknown about a client, and become aware of information gaps that need to be filled.

- Measure progress and redirect attention into service strategies by comparing objectives with performance and learning from experience.

- Correct present service and relationship problems with sounder planning, based on quality client information.

- Better allocate time and talent with advance knowledge of client needs.

- Improve communications among members of the client service team.

- Develop systematic long-range strategies that focus attention on client needs.

- Tailor your services to meet individual client needs, taking into account both long- and short-term client goals.

- Expand total services to desirable existing clients.

- Conduct follow-up evaluations to ensure that articulated goals are being met.

THE CONTENT OF A CLIENT SERVICE PLAN

The actual form a Client Service Plan takes varies from business to business and client to client. Certain elements of the plan are of greater or lesser importance, depending on industry and market considerations. However, the following elements should be incorporated into all Client Service Plans. I will discuss each of these elements in the pages that follow, and I will include examples from actual Client Service Plans.

Client-Firm Reference Data

Client Background Information

This section includes the client's name, address, telephone number, and relevant business statistics, such as the client's total sales volume and total number of employees. An example of the layout is included in Exhibit 6-1.

Exhibit 6-1. Client background information.

Client _____
Address _____
_____
Telephone number_____
Primary SIC Code_____
Sales Volume_____
Employees_____
Fiscal Year_____
Client Since_____

Financial History with Your Firm

A three-year record of total client fees received, broken down by type of service and department is included here. Any billing peculiarities are also recorded. An example of the layout is provided in Exhibit 6-2.

To maximize the potential use of this information, a special subsection can be incorporated

Exhibit 6-2. Financial history with firm.

Year	Total Fees	Services Provided
19__	$_____	Organization Review
19__	$_____	New Product Delivery
19__	$_____	Organization Update

to provide an evaluation of the extent and scope of your services to the client, given its overall financial history.

Key Client Decision Makers

An up-to-date list of key client personnel should be maintained that includes the names, addresses, and telephone numbers of the executive officers, managers, and contact personnel. Additionally, the same information should be compiled for external client personnel, such as the client's attorney, banker, and insurance broker.

The most important resources within any client organization are the key decision makers, with whom you must maintain sound relationships to ensure successful job performance, client retention, and revenue enhancement. This section of the Plan should provide you with biographical notes about these individuals, as well as an up-to-date assessment of your ongoing relationship (or potential relationship) with them. Such data can include items such as birthday and anniversary dates, as well as hobbies and interests.

The following questions need to be answered: Who are the key people we ought to know, but don't? How can we strengthen our relationship with the key people we do know? What should our frequency of contact be with each of these individuals?

Exhibit 6-3 provides an example of how this information has been charted in a Client Service Plan used by one of my clients. Exhibit 6-4 illustrates how frequency of contact is assigned in a Client Service Plan used by a major accounting firm.

Exhibit 6-3. Key client decision makers.

> *Jacob "Jake" Stringer: President.* Jake is a seasoned professional in every sense. He's demanding but fair. He can't abide obtuse communication—simple, direct communication *must* be the norm. Active in his industry association, he reads *Business Marketing*. He is a fair golfer who hates to lose. He is a very close friend of John Buerrant.
>
> *Jerry Brooks: Controller.* Jerry is young and capable. He joined Stringer in 1983 after his father's company (a construction company) folded during the housing recession. He has known Jake for many years through his

Exhibit 6-3. Continued.

father (Larry Brooks). Jerry isn't much of a sportsman and spends his time on community activities instead. He's currently the president of his chapter of the Rotary Club. He's on the Board of Directors of the main chapter of the Atlanta Jaycees.

Hunt Williams: Attorney for Stringer and a member of the Board of Directors. Jack Turner has met Hunt on a couple of occasions, but we know little about him.

Wilma Stringer: Jake's wife and a member of the Board of Directors. She is inactive in company management. She's a tennis enthusiast and we know little else about her.

John Buerrant: Sales Vice President. The leading salesman in Stringer from 1979 through 1985, when he was promoted. He still ranks second to third in sales volume. He is Jake's right-hand man. He's a golfer and loves to travel. We have very little direct contact with him.

Harry Wickes: Materials Manager. He is responsible for making sure inventories are maintained at the right level, shipments go out on time, etc. He's the "production" end of Stringer.

Dan Jenkins: Currently the company's leading salesman. He's only been with Stringer for two years. He's 27 and is definitely a "comer."

Exhibit 6-4. Key client relationship.

Title	**Minimum Contact**
President (Name)	Coordinating partner should contact the president monthly during periods in which we are active with the client in any area of service; should contact the president at least quarterly at other times. Colleague partner should participate once during the closing and in all client satisfaction meetings.
Vice President—Finance	Coordinating partner and management Supervisor should contact the Vice President—Finance at least biweekly when we are engaged in providing a service, and at least bimonthly at all other times.
Controller	Corporate audit manager should contact the controller continually during period of service, and at least monthly at all other times. The audit senior should contact continually as directed by the audit

Exhibit 6-4. Continued.

	manager during the period of service.
Director of Taxes	Tax principal should contact the director of taxes at least once a month.

Network of Relationships

Dual organization charts can be used to identify the crucial relationships and points of contact that occur between your engagement team and client personnel. Exhibit 6-5 shows an example of what a dual organization chart looks like. Within the chart, the quality of each relationship is assessed. A 5 is outstanding, 4 above average, 3 average, 2 below average, and 1 poor.

This chart allows you to keep track of all relevant relationships on every engagement and shows both strengths and weaknesses of the individual relationships.

The Nature of the Client's Operation

This section identifies the critical success factors in the client's industry; it also requires an evaluation of the client's present competitive situation. This evaluation identifies markets served and sought by the client, the client's growth potential in those markets, and client weaknesses.

Exhibit 6-5. Network of relationships.

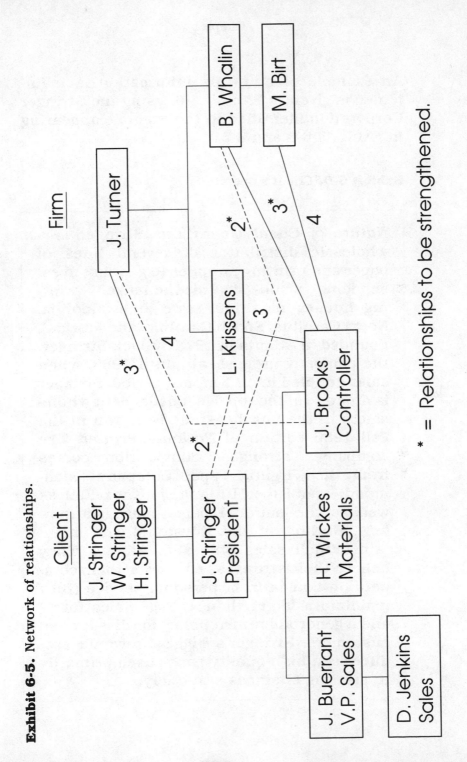

Client

Firm

J. Stringer
W. Stringer
H. Stringer

J. Stringer
President

H. Wickes
Materials

J. Buerrant
V.P. Sales

D. Jenkins
Sales

J. Brooks
Controller

L. Krissens

J. Turner

B. Whalin

M. Birt

3*   4

2*

3

2*

3

3*

4

2*

* = Relationships to be strengthened.

An example of how this information is maintained is given in Exhibit 6-6, using the Stringer Corporation identified in the example appearing in Exhibits 6-3 and 6-5.

Exhibit 6-6. Client's operation.

Nature of Client Operation: Stringer is a wholesale distributor of several lines of paper and printing supplies (e.g., inks, dyes) servicing small- to medium-sized printing houses in a four-state area (Georgia, North Carolina, South Carolina, and Florida). Founded in Atlanta in 1978 by Jack Stringer, the company grew slowly until 1983, when sales doubled in a 12-month period. Stringer is now one of the top five independent wholesalers in the Southeast, as is shown in the Fall 1986 edition of *National Printer*. The company's strongest competition comes from the Virginia Paper Company (Richmond) and Paper Unlimited (Knoxville) as well as the national paper manufacturers (e.g., Burlington and Keystone) who maintain branch sales offices in Atlanta. They believe their strongest edge over their competition comes from personal service (they maintain a larger than average sales force) and a generous return policy for dissatisfied customers. Stringer's biggest revenue producer is a high-quality paper used primarily in printing business stationery.

Client Goals

The identification of your client's short-term and long-term organization and business goals is articulated here. Additionally, the related personal and professional goals of the key decision makers inside the client's firm should be identified.

As an example of how this works, I have included the client goals section of a Client Service Plan prepared by a major consulting firm for a large corporate client after a series of acquisitions resulting from a recent merger (Exhibit 6-7).

Exhibit 6-7. Client's major business goals.

- The client wants to shake down new acquisitions and eliminate loss in its most recent acquisition (where we are presently installing a new standard cost system).
- The client wants to dispose of the company's interest in the synthetic fuels division.
- It is necessary to trim back on operations in those divisions with deteriorating sales.
- The client wants to minimize investment in inventories and receivables and generally conserve cash.
- In the long term, the client would like to acquire a second line of business that is

Exhibit 6-7. Continued.

> counter-cyclical to its present products and not so dependent on energy.
>
> - In the present fiscal year the client hopes to maintain sufficient profitability to satisfy stockholders and earn maximum incentive compensation for management.
> - Next year, after the consolidation process is complete, the client would like to return to historical rates of growth and profitability improvement.
> - The client is proud of its identity as a publicly owned company and wants to maintain that identity.

Client's Current Business Concerns

This section provides an evaluation of problems that must be overcome for the client to achieve its goals. Special subsections can include financial planning, tax considerations, business operations, industry trends, and local concerns. Again referring to the corporation in Exhibit 6-7, I have used material from that client to illustrate the concerns identified in the Client Service Plan (Exhibit 6-8).

Exhibit 6-8. Client's current business problems and concerns.

> - Better management personnel are needed for some of the new acquisitions—Ajax and Demo.

- Systems for determining product profitability and distribution of products need to be improved.
- Adequate records are not available prior to the disposal of certain divisions to make sure that book values reflect all assets.
- Administrative costs will need to be controlled in handling anticipated terminations.
- In order to maximize cash savings, corporate level controls over investment need to be strengthened.
- A suitable acquisition for a second line of production needs to be targeted.

Opportunities For Expanding Service

Both short-term and long-term opportunities should be identified based on an awareness of client needs and operations, and on the evaluation of the services presently being employed by the client. This section would address the following questions: What is the client doing within its own organization to overcome the problems identified above (i. e., Exhibit 6-8)? How can our firm be of assistance in solving those problems?

At the time of preparing your Client Service Plan, it is unlikely that all engagement team members will have been aware of all of the concerns enumerated in the previous section. Some of the opportunities for expanding services that you will investigate might thus entail some additional fact finding and research. You learn as you go in this process. Preparation of Client Alert Reports is a great help in identifying expanded service opportunities.

Obviously the client will have problems and concerns beyond those you have enumerated, but you should limit your focus to those areas that provide you with the potential for expanding service. The nature of previously identified problems is further defined as you move toward an exploration of potential service solutions.

As a general goal, your engagement team will want to enhance relationships at all levels to lay the groundwork for any additional services that are needed, and to demonstrate your continued interest in the client.

Action Recommendations

Specific actions must be identified in order to capitalize on opportunities discussed above. These recommendations can be subdivided into six categories, which include (1) activities to improve and expand relationships, (2) activities to expand services, (3) activities to create and expand referrals, (4) activities to leverage relationships, (5) actions to mesh other disciplines in the office, and (6) actions to upgrade staff.

The *action recommendations* in Exhibit 6-9 are taken from a Client Service Plan used by an accounting firm that wanted to improve and expand relationships with a Key client.

Exhibit 6-9. Action recommendations.

- Paul Fitzpatrick will work with senior staff during the upcoming audit to find ways to better track production costs. Target date: December.

- Bill Samuels will build stronger contacts with Hab Sr., and will extend invitations for two dinners or golf games in the next 12 months. Target date: Winter/Spring.

- Bill Samuels will establish primary relationship with Hab Jr., and will try to meet him socially four times in the next 12 months. Target date: Ongoing.

- Paul Fitzpatrick will improve relations with Hab Jr. To do so, he will meet to discuss general business matters that are not audit related two or three times in the next 12 months. Target date: Ongoing.

- Samuels and Fitzpatrick will meet with Hab Sr. and Hab Jr. to discuss management letter and ideas for (a) better cash utilization and (b) better ways to track production costs. Target date: March/April.

- Millie King will meet with Mike Jurgenson to discuss his personal tax needs. She will

Exhibit 6-9. Continued.

- follow up the contact twice in the next 12 months. Target date: March.
- Millie King will check on progess in completing the responsibilities identified above. Target date: April.
- Paul Fitzpatrick will schedule lunch with Tom Benson to discuss mutual interests and other clients. Target date: May.
- Bill Samuels will arrange and hold a client satisfaction meeting with Hab Jr. & Sr. Target date: May/June.
- Fitzpatrick and King will meet with the loan officer holding the Acme account to determine if the need for certified statements still exists. Target date: June/July.
- Samuels & Fitzpatrick will meet with Hab Jr. & Sr. to discuss the possibility of going to unaudited financials. Target date: Fall.
- Millie King will update pages one through three of the Client Service Plan for next year's planning session. Target date: Fall.

Evaluation and Review

This section will be used to record what contacts have been made, the results of those contacts, and recommendations for future actions in view of the results obtained. All actions should be listed, along with a written summary of the results. Any recommended actions that were not undertaken should also be identified, along with the reasons for the failure to take those actions.

Appendixes

Relevant files and correspondence should be kept available for reference. This would include Client Alert Reports, management letters, engagement letters, and known or suspected competition.

GUIDELINES TO USE IN PREPARATION OF A CLIENT SERVICE PLAN

All key members of your client service team must participate to ensure effective client service planning. Your client service team is often larger than the engagement team. It can include industry experts and other specialists who work with the client. The combined knowledge of the team always exceeds the knowledge possessed by a single individual. By working together, the client service team members pool their knowledge and create a synergistic effect. The team members should be brought together to initiate the process and should meet for a minimum of two hours in discussing and developing the plan.

A Client Service Plan should not be a static document, and it should be designed to accommodate the specific concerns and problems that need to be addressed. It is flexible in both content and form. It should also be updated at appropriate intervals.

In some cases, lack of sufficient knowledge about the client inhibits effective client service planning. When this is the case, your first-year plan should build a program for obtaining the needed knowledge.

In the preceding discussion, I have tried to provide examples taken from a wide variety of clients to illustrate how various aspects of the Client Service Plan are used. Exhibit 6-10 is an example of a blank Client Service Plan, prepared for a national accounting firm, that I have found to be extremely helpful in providing the guidelines necessary to initiate your own planning process.

For those of you who want a briefer version of the Client Service Plan I've included a copy of a Client Development Form, which is shown in Exhibit 6-11.

Exhibit 6-10. Client Service Plan: Proposed outline.

Client: _____ SIC # _____

Prepared __/__/__ Reviewed __/__/__ Updated __/__/__

By _____ By _____ By _____

I. SERVICE TEAM

    1. Present: Years on Engagement

        Partner_____ _____

        Audit Mgr/Spvsr_____ _____

        Audit Senior_____ _____

        Tax Manager_____ _____

        Tax Senior_____ _____

        MAS Consultant_____ _____

        Primary Client_____ _____
          Contact

    2. Previous team members requiring mention

II. LAST 3 YEARS FINANCIAL HISTORY

    A. (Total) Fees (by Type of   (19___   (19___   (19___
       Service)

    B. Realization (Recovery)   ___   ___   ___
       by Fee Function

    C. Audit and Accounting Fees ___ ___ ___

       1. Tax   ___ ___ ___

       2. MAS   ___ ___ ___

       3. EDP   ___ ___ ___

       4. Review/Comp   ___ ___ ___

       4. Other   ___ ___ ___

    D. Billing Peculiarities   ___ ___ ___

III. NATURE OF CLIENT'S OPERATION

    A. Critical Success Factors

    B. Business and Industry Success Factors

       1. Sales volume

       2. Location

       3. Type of industry

       4. Specific products

       5. Other/Deadlines

    C. Markets Served (and Sought)—Growth Potential

    D. Target Markets Critical Weaknesses

    E. Key Client Personnel—Names and Phone Numbers

       1. Owner/Partners

       2. President

       3. Vice President

       4. Treasurer/Controller

       5. Director/Directors of other clients/target markets

       6. Other firm alumni

       7. Client executives who are directors of other entities

Exhibit 6-10. Continued.

    F. Key External Personnel—Names, Addresses, and Phone Numbers

       1. Attorney

       2. Banker

       3. Insurance

       4. Other

       5. Indicate family relationships, if any, for above

    G. Services Primarily Given and Their Frequency

       1. 1120

       2. 1120S

       3. 1065

       4. Audit

       5. Review

       6. Compilation

       7. Pension/Profit sharing audits

       8. Valuation studies

    H. Services Rendered by Other Professional Firms

    I. Recent Developments Affecting Client

IV. CLIENT'S MAJOR BUSINESS GOALS (What are they? What evidence do you have?)

    A. Short-Term

    B. Long-Term

V. CLIENT'S CURRENT BUSINESS CONCERNS

    A. Financial

    B. Tax

    C. Operations

    D. Key Trends in Industry/Local Area

VI. IS FINANCIAL PLANNING NEEDED?

VII. IS TAX PLANNING REQUIRED?

    A. Personal

    B. Corporation

VIII. ACTION FOR THIS YEAR

    A. Activities to Improve/Expand Relationships (Specific)

    B. Activities to Expand Services (Specific)

    C. Activities to Create/Expand Referrals

    D. Other Activities to "Leverage" Relationships

    E. Activities to Mesh Other Disciplines in Office

    F. Actions to Upgrade Staff

IX. WHAT ACTIONS LISTED FOR PRIOR YEARS WERE ACTED UPON?

            ACTION   RESULT

    [Reasons for not acting on intended actions]

X. APPENDIXES

    A. Client Alert Reports

    B. Management Letters

Exhibit 6-10. Continued.

    C.   Prospective Client Data Record

    D.   Engagement Letter

    E.   Known/Suspected Competition

Exhibit 6-11. Client Development Form.

The purpose of this form is to increase our knowledge of the client and determine key areas where we may assist the client.

This form is to be completed on all audits, reviews, and compilations.

  I. List the three biggest problems now facing the client:

    a) _____

       _____

    b) _____

       _____

    c) _____

       _____

  II. List three ways in which the client could save money:

    a) _____

       _____

    b) _____

       _____

    c) _____

       _____

  III. List three ways in which the client could increase revenues:

    a) _____

       _____

Developing Client Service Plans

b) _____
_____

c) _____
_____

IV. Indicate the client's single greatest revenue producer:

   a) _____
_____

   b) _____
_____

   c) _____
_____

V. List new businesses or services the client plans to offer:

   a) _____
_____

   b) _____
_____

   c) _____
_____

VI. List the complicated areas of concern regarding the client's taxes:

   a) _____
_____

   b) _____
_____

   c) _____
_____

VII. Do we prepare the officers' tax returns?
(List officers or key employees)

   a) _____
   b) _____
   c) _____

Exhibit 6-11. Continued

VIII. Do the officers need financial planning?

a) _____

b) _____

c) _____

IX. List any new ventures the key officers might be involved in:

a) _____

b) _____

c) _____

Completed by:_____   Date:_____
Reviewed by:_____   Date:_____
Reviewed by:_____   Date:_____

Potential follow-up procedures for new business from this client:
_____
_____
_____
_____
_____
_____
_____
_____
_____
_____
_____
_____
_____

II

CREATING AND PROTECTING CLIENT REVENUE

7

Conducting the Initial Engagement

First impressions tend to be lasting. In conducting initial engagements I always employ this principle: "You never have a second chance to make a favorable first impression."

The initial engagement is a time of testing for both you and the client. The client is looking to see if you are going to be able to deliver against his expectations. He wants you to be able to validate the assumptions that were made during the new business meeting. He wants to see evidence that the services you provide are worth the time, energy, and money he and his company are required to invest.

You, in turn, are testing the client and trying to answer the following questions: What is the potential for this client? Is it going to be a Mega client? Is there potential for growth? Or is this going to be a relationship that simply limps along?

If you are able to validate the client's expectations, then the initial engagement is extremely important as a foundation builder. I like to think of the initial engagement as being somewhat akin to the first date at the beginning of a romantic relationship. You want to manage it carefully in order to make sure that nothing goes wrong, and that all first impressions are positive.

This chapter describes four must-do actions that will go a long way toward helping you lay the groundwork for the building of client-centered relationships.

STRATEGY CONSIDERATIONS

In managing your client-centered marketing program, it is important to remember that you should not invest too much of your discretionary time on clients with limited potential for growth. Instead, you want to target your high-potential clients and leverage your time with them. Your goal is to create and retain Mega, Key, and "A" clients with potential for growth. Therefore, prior to attempting to build a client-centered relationship, you should make sure that the client is worthy of the special attention and concern you must put forth.

FOUR MUST-DO ACTIONS

In order to meet client expectations, there are four must-do actions that provide positive working principles for the conduct of the initial business engagement.

Make No Assumptions

This is the time to take a fresh look at situations that may be familiar to you from previous business practices. In the initial stages of a new engagement, you should strive to understand how decisions are made within the client's organization, and not impose your preconceived notions on the client's organizational procedures. You don't want to walk in the door and be guilty of the "hairdresser mentality"; that is the hairdresser who cuts hair the way he thinks looks best, regardless of his customer's wishes.

Some service professionals start off on the wrong foot in their initial engagements because they fail to understand the responsibilities assigned to client personnel and make false assumptions about the client's way of doing business. This leads to unnecessary confusion and unnecessary errors.

In my practice I conduct a lot of engagements that are designed to help clients develop and establish client-centered marketing programs in their professional service firms. Some of the major stumbling blocks that I frequently encounter are:

- The marketing practice within the firm has not been organized in a manner that enables the client to recognize the major opportunities within its target industries.

- An inadequate marketing information system is in place.

- Client personnel are not interested in marketing and wish that my program would die an early death.

There is an old cliché that to assume opens the possibility of making an ass out of you and me.

I can testify to this. Early in my career I tended to believe what my clients told me. For example, if a client told me "Our marketing goals are in place and generally well understood," I would accept this as a given and proceed in structuring the engagement as though this were a fact. A seasoned consultant and friend of mine, Irv Lazurous, was assisting me in an engagement, and upon hearing a client suggest that the goals were in place he said, "That's great news, Mr. Client. How about showing Dick and me what they look like so we'll be able to tailor our reports to meet your regular formats." This was a masterful remark. It did not challenge the veracity of the client, but it stressed why our seeing the goals would benefit the client. The client hemmed and hawed a bit, then finally said, "Well Irv, they aren't written down, but I'm pretty certain most of the troops know what they are." Irv suggested that one of our early tasks would be to capture them and present them to the personnel for their use. I never forget that lesson—don't assume!

This is just one example of the types of problems I frequently encounter. By making no assumptions and asking innocent, even simple-minded, questions, I find that I am able to smoke out a lot of useful information that I would not obtain if I came in with a heavy-handed approach and tried to dictate solutions immediately. Instead, I ask questions such as: Why is this done in this way? What marketing strategies have you employed prior to undertaking this engagement?

One of my early mentors told me that professionals prove how smart they are not by what they say, but by the manner in which they ask questions and then respond to the answers given by the client. This process of asking simple, probing questions not only helps me to become more informed of client procedures, but also educates the client and helps her to begin to perceive the problems and needs that I have been hired to address.

In general, the investigative, open-ended questions starting with *Who*, *What*, *When*, *Where*, and *Why* are the best probing questions. My goal is to obtain a verbal snapshot of the present situation and the players involved so I can get an early sense of whom and what I have to work with.

Create Interim Wins

Instead of waiting until the end of the engagement to deliver a finalized product, consciously strive to create "deliverables" that give the client something to hold on to. Even though these "deliverables" do not represent finished products, they reinforce the client's original favorable buying decision and beat back any post-purchase doubts or fears.

As an example of how this process works, I recently created an interim organization chart for a new client who was in need of reassurance. In giving him this chart, I told him that the chart represented my initial thinking on the organization needed to create a winning marketing program. I invited him to give me his early impressions regarding the organizational structure and reporting relationships that were spelled out in the chart. He was reassured by seeing my early ideas, and it gave me a further opportunity to elicit information from him. In this case I was able to think along with the client and to discuss his assessments of each of the players I identified in the interim chart. I was also able to glean additional information regarding longer-term plans in order to structure a chart that could be used on possible future organizational moves. Michael and Timothy Mescow, two management psychologists, once said, "It's the aggregation of the little things that make the difference between satisfaction and sadness."

Manage Your Visibility

During the course of an initial engagement, the client is going to be monitoring your performance closely. She wants to know that when your meter is running, she is receiving an appropriate level of value in return. By skillfully managing your visibility, you can demonstrate that you are the type of individual who takes full advantage of the opportunities to obtain information and insight from the client personnel and resources that are made available to you.

Once on the job it is easy to get too busy to seize the opportunities available for "provident proximity." In managing your visibility, your goal is to go about your work in a way that leaves a good impression on the client. One method for doing so is to make it a point to be at the client's offices a bit earlier than the regular employees and to leave a bit later than your client contact. This unspoken behavior demonstrates that you are a hard worker willing to put in the hours necessary to get the job done.

A second method for managing your visibility is to create and take advantage of informal opportunities that allow you to cement your relationship with your client contact. For example, when I'm working on-site, I frequently walk to the parking lot with a client. This gives me the opportunity to talk in a relaxed, informal setting away from ringing telephones and other distractions. It also underscores the fact that I am still on the job when others are leaving the office and makes me visible in a positive yet unobtrusive way. Other simple, timely, and inexpensive things you can do to keep in touch with key client executives during the course of the engagement include the following:

- Schedule lunch with them.
- Go out of your way to say good morning and good night to them.
- Keep them informed on the progress of the engagement.
- Attend company functions when appropriate. For example, I make it a point to attend T.G.I.F. functions with one of my high-potential clients. Sharing a cola-and-chips

celebration is a pleasant way of upgrading a relationship.

- Invite the client to social activities and athletic events.
- Provide client executives with information and publications.
- Time your breaks to coincide with the client's rest breaks and chat over coffee.

You should also make every effort to identify the *players* in the organization and create reasons to introduce yourself to them. In doing so, you should be careful not to give the impression that you are "on the make," eager to spend the client's money by drumming up new business opportunities. Instead, such introductory conversations should focus on needs and information related to the job at hand. If this is not possible, a bit of friendly social discourse is preferable to retiring from the field at this early stage of the relationship.

Finally, a professional service provider should try not to take telephone calls from other clients or prospective clients. This is especially true when you are meeting with your client contact. As basic as this rule seems, I have seen professional consultants violate it frequently. When you are on-site, your time and attention need to be devoted to that individual client and no one else.

If you are working off-site for a client that you believe has the potential to be a Mega, Key, or "A"

client, periodic telephone contact or FAX mes-
sages are good ways to maintain your visibility.
You should continue to let the client know that
you are working on her behalf by giving her informal progress reports. The fact that you are tem-
porarily out of sight does not mean that you need
be out of mind.

Verify Your Results Against Client Expectations

Every initial engagement should conclude with
a Client Satisfaction Meeting. The procedure for
conducting this meeting is described in the section that follows. But you need not wait until
the conclusion of the engagement to obtain
client verification. Rather than take a chance
on last minute upsets or misunderstandings
regarding the final form of the product, you can
do some preliminary checking while your work
is in progress. You can give periodic updates,
saying "This is where I am so far." Then ask,
"Is this on target?" Such an approach helps
to focus client expectations and prevents last
minute surprises.

CONDUCTING THE CLIENT SATISFACTION MEETING

The Client Satisfaction Meeting is an integral
part of a client-centered marketing program that
is built into the initial engagement. The purpose of the meeting is to obtain feedback from
client executives regarding their perceptions of

the nature and quality of the relationship and the service that has been provided to them. It is also an excellent time to plant "seeds of need" for future business and to create referrals.

The procedure for conducting the meeting is simple and straightforward. To begin, what you want to do is ask, then listen to and discuss the client's responses to these questions:

- What is your opinion of our firm and services?

- What is your opinion of the members of our firm with whom you had contact?

- To what extent do you feel that we were prompt and kept you informed?

- Have our services assisted you in areas other than those specified in the engagement?

- Are there areas in which you have been disappointed by our job performance?

- Would you be willing to recommend us to other people if asked?

After initiating the discussion by soliciting client opinions and listening to the responses, you want to give the client feedback regarding your experience. You can mention pluses and minuses and discuss any problems that arose. Your aim is to develop constructive candor on both sides of the client/consultation equation. It is best to admit mistakes and discuss any potentially troublesome issues before they disrupt the relationship.

In discussing your job performance, you can make client benefits visible by having the client verify that job performance goals have been met. If you did a good job in formulating your letter of agreement before the job started, then verification of job performance is simpler. In your meeting, you simply present your results against the stated agreement, and have the client's decision-making team give you a verbal sign-off that conveys their satisfaction that the stated job criteria have been met.

Ideally, you should strive to come in under budget on the first job. The strategy is to bid comfortably, and then come in on time and under budget while meeting or exceeding all of the client's expectations. In so doing, you should make it a point to show clients the savings that have accrued, so that they are aware of precisely what you have done.

If the client affirms that things went well during the engagement, then this is a good time to introduce a possible need for future business discussions. You can do so by saying, "As I was completing the engagement, I recognized [state client need or problem]. I think I can be of some help to you in this area. Is this something that you would be interested in talking about?" This is a casual type of comment; you are not trying to come on strong and make the sale at that moment, but creating the opportunity for future sales discussions.

EVALUATING THE CLIENT

At the conclusion of your initial engagement, you need to evaluate the client and ask yourself: Does this client warrant additional service and attention?

Every time you bring a new client aboard, you hope that it has the potential to become a Mega, Key, or A client. After the initial engagement, some of these clients are easy to spot. You may have found, for example, that things went smoothly throughout the course of the engagement, that the client's top people were willing to listen to your recommendations, and that they asked questions that gave you an opportunity to introduce the need for additional services. Other clients are not so easy to read at first. They may be cautious and reluctant to reveal their true feelings. Still others are not in sync with you, your program, or your recommendations. They may try to nickel and dime you to death by asking for freebies and extra effort on your part. One favorite strategy of such clients is to try to change or widen the scope of the agreement during the engagement. Chapter 10 will cover ways you can handle this. For now, the important point is that in order to leverage your time, you need to make a decision regarding the potential of your client.

One method for making this decision is to compare the client with client characteristics discussed in Chapter 2. By evaluating a client according to these characteristics after the completion of the initial engagement, you can classify that client as a Mega, Key, A, B, C, or D client. This will give you a baseline that will enable you to leverage your time in making future decisions. The goal is to maximize revenue in the management of your client base.

To meet this objective you want to maximize the amount of time and attention you devote to your highly desirable clients, minimizing the amout of time devoted to undesirable clients. Too often marginal clients receive A-level attention. The hope of the service provider is that somehow these D-level relationships will improve. But the truth is that D clients seldom change, and in order to leverage time it is necessary to identify candidates for termination as well as targets for special attention and concern.

8

Selling Additional Services to Existing Clients

When properly managed, existing clients represent your own captive market. You have earned the right to be heard, and these clients will listen to your ideas for improving their performance. If you do not capitalize on the opportunities inherent in this relationship by serving all the client needs you are equipped to handle, there is a strong probability that the client will go elsewhere to obtain services that you are capable of providing.

In laying the groundwork for expanding the services that you provide to an existing client, you do not want to be in a frame of mind where you are asking yourself: How do I sell additional services to client X? Rather, you should strive to get the client to see that you've got answers to problems that will help her do better in producing the outputs that she is in business to produce. You do this by asking, "In what ways can I assist this client in doing better what she is in business to do?"

Exhibit 8-1 graphically portrays the major elements involved in selling additional services. In the pages that follow I will discuss several of the more essential ideas within the elements.

SETTING THE STAGE

Goal

The goal is to provide additional profitable services to receptive existing clients with needs

Exhibit 8-1. Selling additional services to existing clients.

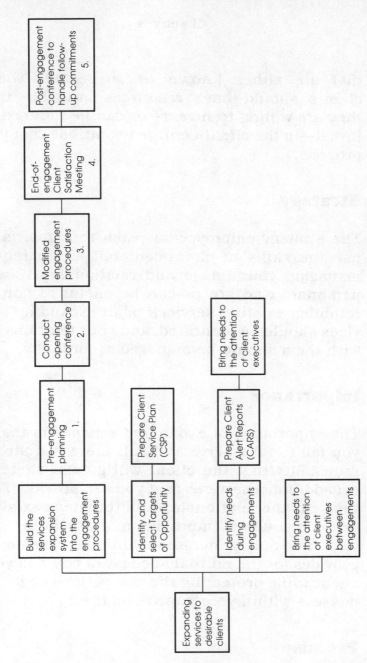

that are either known or suspected. These clients should have resources available that they are willing to invest—or can be induced to invest—in the client-centered solutions that you propose.

Strategy

The strategy employed to reach this goal is to use the skills of client-centered marketing in managing your image and relationship. Client personnel who are or can be useful to you in retaining existing services or in expanding services should be identified, and your relationship with them should be managed accordingly.

Importance

The importance of expanding services is that if you fail to fully serve a client, there is a strong probability that the client will go elsewhere to get additional services that you can provide. This weakens the relationship and threatens existing revenue sources. Improving and expanding services not only generates additional revenue, it provides for the mutual success of you and your client while protecting the competitive edge you possess within your captive market.

Premise

As I mentioned earlier, your goal is not to sell additional services, but to assist the client in achieving his objectives through the appropriate use of your resources. Your role should be to guide the client to recognize the value and importance of the resources you can provide. Selling additional services will be a natural outgrowth of this client-centered approach.

Barriers

In trying to expand the range of services your firm provides to a targeted client, you will routinely encounter several barriers. These barriers must be identified and then overcome. Typically, barriers that inhibit your firm's ability to generate new sources of revenue from existing clients include both organizational and personnel factors. Some of the most common barriers are identified in Exhibit 8-2.

Exhibit 8-2. Organizational and personnel barriers.

Organizational Barriers

1. There is a lack of coordination and communication between departments.
2. The selling of additional services is not valued (or rewarded) as highly as bringing in new clients.
3. Firm employees are not sufficiently trained.
4. Engagements are bid too tight, with the result that your client-engagement team does not have enough time to do research and plant seeds.

Exhibit 8-2. Continued.

> 5. Insufficient staffing of the client-engagement team.
>
> *Personnel Barriers*
>
> 1. Client-engagement personnel are not expected to sell additional services.
> 2. Firm employees in the field do not know how to sell additional services.
> 3. Employees know how to sell additional services, but fail to do so because:
>   (a) they fear rejection
>   (b) an adequate reward/punishment program is not in place
>   (c) they are too busy with other tasks
>   (d) they have an adversary relationship with clients
>   (e) they have an adversary relationship with personnel in other departments.
> 4. Firm employees have not properly educated clients about the benefits that can be derived from additional services.
> 5. Firm employees are resistant to change and prefer to go on doing things in the "traditional" manner.

The solution to most of these barriers is to make selling additional services a requirement for continued employment with the firm. To illustrate how this can be done, I will discuss each item identified in Exhibit 8-2.

Organizational Barriers

1. *There is a lack of coordination and communication between departments.* This can be a problem with firms that still have an *ad hoc* marketing function. For example, accounting firms have three major departments: accounting, tax, and management advisory services. Unless there is a policy for ensuring coordination among them, the major department assumes the primary responsibility for servicing the client. The result is that the audit partner often winds up with a disproportionate amount of control. The solution is to appoint a *client services partner*, who should be the person who *best* knows the full range of the client's needs. All Mega, Key, and A clients should have a Client Service Plan prepared, and the CAR should be used on every engagement, with the client service partner supervising this process.

   One firm I worked with schedules full staff luncheon meetings and serves pizza while various assignments designed to improve communications and coordination are completed. I have found such informal working luncheons to be extremely beneficial as a way of increasing communication. I once conducted a "Build a Marketing Information System" meeting during a lunch session. The troops were required to attend and to bring their client files and

Rolodexes. In this informal setting, several extremely important issues surfaced that might well have been ignored if the troops had not been brought together for this meeting.

2. *The selling of additional services is not valued (or rewarded) as highly as bringing in new clients.* This situation is common in service firms. The thrill of the chase and the hope that the new clients will be today's and tomorrow's winner burns brightly in most of us. The solution to this is to build cross-selling of another department's services into the career appraisal and development process. A management consulting client of mine solved this problem quickly and easily by making every staff person on every engagement responsible for uncovering at least one new client need. They were required to report on the new need during the Friday meeting in the office. An old management maxim holds true: "What gets measured and rewarded for success, and punished for failure, gets done!"

3. *Firm employees are not sufficiently trained.* This barrier continues to exist in too many firms. The notion is that somehow the troops will learn how to do this, and that marketing is "soft" training. Furthermore, it's hard to track the resulting lost revenues. The more enlightened firms provide both basic and advanced training on a regular basis. I've noticed a surge in the number of courses offered by

associations and firms in marketing and client service. An inexpensive approach is to purchase a good marketing book and to conduct cracker barrel discussion sessions during lunch or breakfast meetings.

4. *Engagements are bid too tight, with the result that your client-engagement team does not have enough time to do research and plant seeds*. This often happens with the smaller engagements. But with large, desirable clients can you afford not to do the necessary research and seed planting? The solution to this situation is to force the preparation of the CARs during the engagement, and to convene the service team in order to prepare the Client Service Plan.

5. *Insufficient staffing of the client-engagement team*. This problem, when coupled with barrier number 4, is virtually impossible to correct. The result is that the client is poorly served, and the problem goes away when the client leaves the firm. The most common staffing problems are (a) too few staff to do the grunt work, which winds up being done by the more expensive troops, which leads to poor realization; and (b) staff so new that they still have tunnel vision and pass by client needs. In both cases, engagement performance suffers unnecessarily. Once again, a policy and enforcement procedure for mandating the preparation of the Client Service Plan and CARs for desirable clients is the primary step toward a solution.

145

Personnel Factors

1. *Client engagement personnel are not expected to sell additional services.* The obvious first step in solving this problem is to make the selling of additional services a requirement for continued employment with the firm, and then to build in systems for ensuring that the Client Service Plan and CARs are prepared.

2. *Firm employees in the field do not know how to sell additional services.* This is the direct result of organizational barrier number 3, and as that barrier is handled on an organizational basis, this personnel problem should begin to clear up. Of course, the quality of training and the nature and regularity of reinforcement and management review are determinants of whether this problem gets solved.

3. *Employees know how to sell additional services, but fail to do so because:*

    (a) *They fear rejection.* This can be solved by providing training. But let's face it; some people are just not up to the job of direct, face-to-face new business development. If such an employee is truly valued, you might get by with using him to manage the CSP and to turn in CARs. The problem with this approach is that you tacitly approve of an exception to the policy you have put in place.

(b) *An adequate reward/punishment program is not in place.* This goes back to the need for a policy that is installed and enforced. Some firms do not have the guts to invoke sanctions, for fear of losing their employees. The result is that money is lost as additional service opportunities are squandered.

(c) *They are too busy with other tasks.* This is too often true in firms that are thinly staffed, and it shows up in organizational barrier number 5. The only solution is to set priorities for "must-do" tasks, which include selling additional services and servicing other client needs.

(d) *They have an adversary relationship with clients.* This can be allowed to happen only once—the first time is always the last! It's a fact of life that some clients and servers, like oil and water, do not mix. But if there is a pattern of bad relations between an employee and a client, your employee must be taken off the engagement or you will lose your client.

(e) *They have an adversary relationship with personnel in other departments.* The answer to this is organizational in principle and personal in practice. The two warring parties must be made to see that the service of the client comes before any departmental issue. In firms where one department wags the tail, this is an ever-present problem. For years, the accountants used to have such a position in some of the Big 8 accounting firms. Increased competition and the emergence of the consulting operation as a big revenue producer, however, have turned this around.

4. *Firm employees have not properly educated clients about the benefits that can be derived from additional services.* This usually occurs because they do not know the full range of services the firm can provide, or it arises from a combination of organizational and personal barriers. The solution is to convene interdepartmental meetings to discuss the range of services available in each department and to identify indicators of the need for such services.

5. *Firm employees are resistant to change and prefer to go on doing things in the traditional manner.* Fortunately, this situation does not last long. The pace of change is accelerating, and these employees soon find themselves out of the public practice area. Resistance to change is often linked to insufficient knowledge and skills. Basic training coupled with good policies can bring about improvements that help to overcome this barrier.

ACTIVATING THE PROCESS

Building Marketing into the Engagement Process

Your client-centered marketing program should be built into your engagement process. In examining Exhibit 8-1, you can see that this is a five-stage process. At each stage the professional service provider encounters marketing opportunities and responsibilities.

The process starts with pre-engagement planning. Here you want to review relevant Client Service Plans and Client Alert Reports to examine new business leads. Some of these leads might require additional work and research, which should be incorporated into your pre-engagement planning.

The next stage is the entrance conference. At this conference you meet with the client to begin the engagement, and you review the job performance criteria that define the scope of the engagement. In identifying client expectations, it is important to be as specific as possible so that the scope of the engagement is not arbitrarily expanded. Any significant additional responsibilities you take on should result in a modification of your initial agreement letter.

The third stage is the actual conduct of the engagement. During the performance of your job responsibilities, your strategy is to manage your visibility in such a way that the client feels he is getting value from your services. Several tips on how to do so have been included on pages 128–132 in Chapter 7. From a procedural point of view the important point is that by managing your visibility you enhance your potential for generating additional sources of revenue. This marketing aspect of job performance, which is frequently overlooked and undervalued, is designed to allow you to leverage your time and operate within your comfort zone.

At the conclusion of the engagement, you conduct a Client Satisfaction Meeting, where you determine the level of client satisfaction with your services, solicit referrals, and plant the seeds of future need. When future (or additional) client needs are ready for discussion, the Client Satisfaction Meeting will often extend into a post-engagement conference, where you propose additional services, identify solutions to client problems, and start the entire process rolling once again.

The Policy Statement

The rationale for bringing additional needs to the attention of a client should be established in the first new business meeting you have with a prospective client. When you talk about firm policy in that meeting, you can inform the client that your firm's policy is to bring items of interest that you discover to the client's attention. For example, you might say: "Our firm's service philosophy is to be alert to ways in which we can assist you in the conduct of your business. If we discover any problem areas during the course of our engagement, we will bring them to your attention."

The purpose of such a policy statement is to establish the basis for additional services. When the time comes to make known to the client your willingness to meet additional needs that you have identified, you can refer to the previously stated policy as a nonthreatening way of introducing the subject. This increases the size of your comfort zone and eliminates the element of surprise.

Spotting Needs during the Engagement

The key to selling additional services to existing desirable clients is to look for leads in the right places during the engagement. In this section I identify four ways to spot needs. They are:

- Client Service Plans
- Client Alert Reports
- Eyeballing the situation
- Examining recent engagements for clients in a similar industry

Client Service Plans

The components of a Client Service Plan were discussed in detail in Chapter 6. When properly put into practice, Client Service Plans will provide you and members of your service team with a number of ideas to explore and needs to examine. They should be kept up-to-date through periodic revision and made an integral part of your pre-engagement planning.

Client Alert Reports

These reports were discussed in Chapter 5. Recall that the purpose of the CAR is to identify and bring to the attention of the engagement partner evidence of unmet or poorly met client needs and problems, as well as other client-related factors that could affect the relationship. Pre-engagement planning should emphasize the importance of CARs. The following steps are helpful in maximizing the potential value of these reports during the course of your engagements.

- Allow time on budget for preparation of CARs.
- Alert staff to keep eyes and ears open, and to be aware of any problem areas.
- Research and become aware of services your firm provides to similar clients.
- Make filing of CARs mandatory for every member of the client engagement team.
- Perform analytical review, comparing client to industry trends for several periods, to identify potential problem areas.

While the engagement is in progress, Client Alert Reports should be submitted by the staff for review by the client engagement manager. When necessary, you can probe for additional data and tighten the leads prior to making a recommendation for action.

Eyeballing the Situation

An experienced professional can spot client needs by eyeballing the client's equipment, office procedures, and personnel. In my early days of learning how to consult, I visited client organizations with a seasoned consultant, who used the notion of giving the situation a "smell test." As we walked through a corridor to a client's shipping dock, he spotted a number of broken pallets to be used in transporting the products the client prepared. He turned to me and said, "There is a quality control engagement just begging to be sold here. Let's go in and get it." Later, during a lull in the conversation that occasioned our visit, he remarked to the client, "It seems to me that you may have a problem in the making out in your shipping dock. Have you noticed what's going on out there?"

By not telegraphing the problem, he caught the client's attention, and the client was listening when he went on to say, "Given the number of busted pallets you have got lying around, it appears to me that you have a serious quality control situation. Do you have any idea of what this is costing you?" The client responded by saying that he thought a certain amount of breakage was normal, and then he asked the consultant what he thought. The consultant indicated that he would look into the situation and get back to the client with his recommendations. As it turned out, he was able to institute a quality control program that saved his client thousands of dollars.

This is a good example of when and how to bring a need to the attention of a client while you are eyeballing the premises. By keeping your eyes and ears open while you are on-site, you can frequently find problems that result in inefficient business practices. These problems should be brought to the client's attention, along with a discussion of possible solutions.

Recent Engagements

Recent engagements done for other clients in the same industry provide another valuable, yet inexpensive, source of leads. You can verify a suspected need by telling your current client: "I've been thinking about your [need you want to bring to her attention]. I recently completed an assignment for a client in your industry that resulted in [the benefits he achieved through the use of your firm]. I wanted to check this out with you. Is this something you would be interested in?"

Bringing Needs to the Client's Attention

I am often asked about the best way to bring client needs to a client's attention. Unfortunately, there is no hard and fast rule that is applicable to all business situations.

Raising these issues does occasionally stir anxiety in some people because they feel they are venturing into uncharted territory and fear rejection. Therefore, it is best to bring client needs to the client's attention in a low-key conversational manner. Don't rush into a hard sell or trap the client when she is preoccupied with other matters. Instead, think of planting your seeds of need in much the same way one would extend a social invitation.

For example, over lunch you might say: "I noticed that some of the staff are spending a lot of time on Project X, and they seem to be frustrated by a lack of data input and retrieval. Is this something that you were aware of?" If the client expresses an interest in what you've discovered, then you might provide her with a brief description of how you would handle the problem. This pre-sells the idea and opens the door for more formal business discussions.

Many people fail to recognize that they can open client needs for discussion during the course of an ongoing engagement. They prefer to wait until the engagement has been completed. But it is often more difficult to get the client's attention after the engagement has been completed. If it looks as if you are going to earn a recurring relationship, it is best to keep the lines of communication open on a regular informal basis, as well as on a formal basis.

In order to increase the size of your comfort zone in doing so, you should bring needs to a client's attention only after you've got your facts down. This is not a time for a fishing expedition. Instead, you should be able to state clearly what the problem is and how the client will be better off once the need is addressed.

Selling Extensions

Once needs have been identified and brought to the attention of the client, you are often in a position to sell extensions to the present engagement. This means that you have the opportunity to expand the scope of the work during the engagement that is already in progress. In Chapter 10 I will discuss tactics that can be used to keep you from giving scope changes away. For now, it is important to underscore the fact that every request for additional coverage on the current engagement presents you with an opportunity to modify the letter of agreement or write a new one.

Cross-Selling

Cross-selling refers to the activity of one person selling the need for services offered by a person in a different specialty area or another department. If the initiating professional has a good grasp of the benefits of the recommended service, it is okay for her to move into the problem definition step. Usually, however, the initiator's task is to obtain sufficient information so she can pass on the information to the next professional, who then meets with the client. As with all new business discussions, the key to success is to be very specific in what you are proposing in terms of the need and the benefits to be gained by the client. Bringing in the other professionals from your firm to discuss a need situation is an accepted method with few negatives attached.

9

Creating and Managing a Client Referral System

Creating and maintaining strong client referrals is an essential client-centered marketing task. Good, active client referral sources make your marketing task easier because they:

- Enable you to make contacts with preconditioned prospective clients who are generally more receptive to meeting with you because of their regard for the person making the referral.

- Enable you to acquire an insider's understanding of their industry/profession because you have the opportunity to discuss changes, trends, and needs in their area of operations.

- Enable you to develop additional business contacts while working within your comfort zone, thus eliminating much of the resistance that is often encountered in other, more aggressive marketing environments.

THE ANATOMY OF A REFERRAL

It is helpful sometimes to look at the psychological structure of a referral situation. This is usually a four-step process. Each of those steps will now be described.

1. *The Key client's needs and expectations are met or exceeded, and she appreciates this fact.* For example, many of my service firm clients make it a policy to exceed the scope of the promised *deliverables* on engagements with their best clients.

With my best clients I do this by tightly defining the need and the deliverables necessary to meet that need. I then present more deliverables than were bargained for, and thus exceed the original expectations. Recently, I was serving a PR firm that had grown rapidly and had virtually no marketing or selling systems in place. My initial engagement was to work with the client's computer people in developing a computerized client and referral tracking system. In addition to installing the system and training the computer people, I offered a freebie to the executives when I gave them several of my own tracking elements for their use. My client contact was very happy with this, as were the firm's executives.

2. *In many well-served clients, a sense of pride sets in.* Pride is integrally related to a job well done. The client will begin to think, "I have an eye for hiring good people who like to serve me." As a consequence of the engagement, her self-esteem will be increased.

3. *A sense of fair play is triggered, and the client experiences a desire to reciprocate.* In the case of the PR firm cited above, where the executives were provided with my own tracking elements, the client was immediately receptive to my request to have him serve as a "vouch-for" for me. I knew I had someone I could use as a reference point whenever the need arose.

4. *The client begins to tell others about you and initiates referrals.* This isn't an un-

selfish act on the client's part. Many times it is a disguised way to tell the world, "In this dog-eat-dog environment, I have the ability to acquire consulting assistance that truly serves me and I want you to know about it." It is also a way for the client to reward a valued asset, namely you, and it ensures that the working relationship will continue.

The bottom line of the referral situation is that in order to obtain referrals, you need to meet or exceed client expectations and the client needs to be aware that you have done so. Once the client's expectations have been met or exceeded, a principle begins to operate that I call the North American sense of fair play.

The client begins to say to himself, "Wow, I'm getting a wonderful deal from this guy." Automatically, he starts to feel good about himself, and on a psychological level is thinking, "Boy, I know how to pick good people in this day and age of slick marketing techniques and rip-off artists." That builds his confidence and self-esteem.

Simultaneously, his sense of fair play is triggered and he wants to reciprocate. He's thinking, "I need to balance this relationship out." In short, he wants to move from a vertical relationship to a level relationship. He knows he can do so by sharing the news of your talents with other significant professionals. At that point, he is ready to become a 24-hour unpaid salesperson working on your behalf.

Goal

The goal of establishing a client referral program is to expand the number of your unpaid salespersons; that is, existing and previous clients who provide you with leads, speak well of you, and invite you to their professional affairs. By definition, your Mega, Key, and "A" clients are good clients and you like to serve them. These people tend to associate with business professionals of a similar caliber, and obtaining referrals from them provides you with an opportunity to clone existing Mega, Key, and "A" clients.

Premise

The best time to begin developing client referrals is at an early stage of your relationship, when you are conducting the Client Satisfaction Meeting. At this meeting client needs and expectations surface, and you make *visible* to the client how and where you met or exceeded her expectations. Client awareness of these benefits is essential to obtaining client referrals.

A client who makes referrals is designated as Key and warrants a special relationship that must be nurtured and protected. After the initial problems have been handled, most clients and professionals tend to drift into an "arm's-length" relationship. Thus, it is essential to provide a continuing *care-and-feeding* program that allows you to maintain contact between engagements.

I learned about the importance of care-and-feeding programs when I served as Director of Training and Development for an international consulting firm. Prior to starting the first engagement with a new client, the partners of this firm would tell the client, "Your mailbox will never be empty once we begin to work with you. We pride ourselves on keeping you informed about new developments within your area of interest and within our firm."

Based on this experience, I have since devised my own care-and-feeding program for my consulting practice. The major steps I use in this program include the following.

- I immediately address five envelopes with the name and address of my key client contact and put them in my pending file for the next month's actions. This has a positive effect since I detest missing deadlines. Seeing the envelope forces me to think of something the client should know, and having it addressed makes it easy for me to complete the task.

- I read extensively and tear out pages of management-related articles and comments, which I will often send to clients along with a brief, handwritten note. This lets the client know that I was thinking of her, and helps keep her informed of items of mutual interest.

- With a few of my best clients, I have developed a partnership relationship of the kind I described earlier. I will ask these clients for advice about new business opportunities, new services, and market conditions. This establishes a degree of reciprocity in the flow of information and keeps the relationship level, rather than putting me in the exalted position of being the sole expert.

- I'm not an entertainment type, but I do occasionally arrange to meet a client for breakfast or lunch.

- I make it a point to maintain periodic telephone contact with clients, even though I may not be involved in an ongoing engagement. Every so often a client will tell me, "I'm glad you called. Something just came up that you should be included in." I have a PR client who will seldom call me, but who has never sounded rushed when I call him. I recently called him to check out a detail for some work to be done later this year, and I ended up booking several hours of work I would not have got if I had not called. My consultant friends tell me this is a common, and delightful, occurrence.

Advantages and Benefits

A strong, well-functioning referral program has numerous advantages over other marketing techniques. These include:

1. Satisfied clients have first-hand knowledge of the services your firm provides and can communicate this knowledge to other professionals in an "objective" manner that is not tainted by self-interest.

2. You are often pre-sold.

3. The previously established relationship results in low-cost marketing when you follow up on client referrals.

4. No hard sell is required. A client referral allows you to work well within the range of your comfort zone.

5. A satisfied, reputable client active in the business community is a low-cost form of advertising that enhances your self-esteem.

6. Satisfied clients create an *exposure network*, which enhances your firm's reputation and increases the number of potential business relationships.

7. A client referral reduces the need for ice breaking and allows you to leverage your time.

Problems in Using Referrals

The use of referrals is usually an effective marketing strategy, but it does have potential drawbacks that you should be aware of. Some of the disadvantages are that

- A referring client might oversell your services, making promises on which you cannot (or do not want to) deliver.

- The prospective client may be suspicious of the motives of the referral source.

- The prospective client may not respect the referral source, and therefore your reputation might be damaged by association with the referring client.

In order to minimize these problems, it is important to be aware that you can educate clients on what you want them to say. The referral sources are trying to act in your best interest, but sometimes they might get carried away and overpromise. The first time you get them to make a referral, you can describe the types of clients you are looking for and the type of referral that you feel is appropriate.

I have developed a simple educational approach to get my client thinking along the lines that will help him to help me. I tell him, "Mr. Client, one of the reasons I enjoy working with you is [I define an aspect of the client relationship that I enjoy, such as the way he listens and responds to my ideas, or his willingness to maintain a level relationship]. In addition, the size and vitality of your organization are typical of the clients that we prefer to work with and that we feel we do a good job of serving. When your colleague organizations have a need for our type of services, I'd appreciate your telling them about us. Do any names come to mind at this time?"

In soliciting referrals, you want to manage them to ensure that they come from high-quality clients who are respected within the industry or profession being served.

To maintain a strong referral base it is important to be aware of the psychology involved in giving referrals. Just as a client may feel he is getting a wonderful benefit and therefore wants to even out the relationship prior to giving you a referral, he can also feel used if you begin to take him for granted or if you use him too often. Therefore, it is important to maintain multiple referral sources and to reward those that give you referrals with expressions of gratitude and other appropriate forms of appreciation.

Classes of Client Referrals

There are two classes of clients who offer referrals on your firm's behalf: initiators and vouch-fors.

Initiators are clients who actively make referrals on your behalf. They provide you with leads, invite you to meet their colleagues, and generally serve as unpaid sales representatives who find value in promoting you and your firm.

Initiators are made, not born. They generally come from clients who recognize and appreciate the fact that you have exceeded their expectations, and they are strong enough and confident enough to actively promote you. For a relationship that has been elevated to a partnership level, the odds are high that the client is initiating new business for the server.

Vouch-fors are clients that let you use their name and will respond favorably to inquiries made by prospective clients, but they seldom undertake actions to initiate referrals.

BUILDING A REFERRAL SYSTEM

There are three basic steps required to initiate a marketing referral system.

1. Inventory your existing Key client referral sources.

2. Develop an action plan for relationship development.

3. Expand your base of client referral sources.

Inventory

It is important to know where you are before you can decide where you want to go. The first step is to take stock of your present situation. To do so, you should maintain an inventory of all existing and recent clients who do or do not make referrals on your behalf. Exhibit 9-1 provides a worksheet that can be used in such an inventory.

After identifying those clients that do make referrals, you should classify the type of referrals made. Are they initiators, vouch-fors, or a combination of both? In your inventory, you should maintain a record of the frequency of the referrals made. This allows you to assign a grade to each client that initiates referrals or has done

Exhibit 9-1. Existing Key client referral sources.

Client Executives Name and Affiliation	Initiate?		QOR† (1 to 5)	Potential**		How Do I Plan to Use This Referral Source
	N	Y*		Short-Term	Long-Term	

*Level of effort
A = continuing/recurring
B = sporadic
C = one time only/dormant

†QOR = Quality of Relationship
1 = Low
5 = Perfect

**Potential
H = High
M = Medium
L = Low

so in the past: A is for a continuing/recurring referral source, B for a sporadic referral source, and C for a one-time-only referral source or one that has gone dormant.

This inventory worksheet should be completed for all clients that compose your existing client base. It should be updated on a periodic basis so you can keep track of progress being made or any backsliding that occurs.

Once your inventory is complete, you will want to consider the following questions.

- How many of my Key clients actually make referrals at this time?
- Why are these clients making referrals?
- Why are some of my best clients not making referrals?
- How frequently do I contact referral sources to thank them for their efforts?
- How often do I actively seek referrals? And to whom do I turn when I do so?
- How many referral sources do I have in my primary, high-potential markets?

An Action Plan for Relationship Development

Earlier in the book I said that business development is relationship development. This principle is particularly true concerning the cultivation and expansion of a referral base. To obtain referrals from clients, you need to value the relationships you develop throughout the course of your practice and do what you can to enhance the quality of those relationships. Like all forms of marketing, this requires investing nonbillable time and occasional sacrifice, but when properly done the end result is new business and revenue enhancement.

I have developed a ten-step action plan to help you identify potential referral sources and put in motion a program to use them.

1. Establish an "acquaintance account" that identifies potential referral sources. These sources include both existing clients and non-client influentials. In identifying non-client influentials, you might want to consider previous business contacts, social contacts, and college alumni.

2. After identifying specific individuals, write each name down on a 3 × 5 card. Beneath their names identify (1) what you can do for them, and (2) what they can do for you.

3. Classify each individual, according to the markets you are trying to reach, as (a) influential in your target market, (b) potentially influential in your target market, or (c) noninfluential in your target market.

4. Delete from your card file all cards that receive a *c* rating in step 3.

5. For each card that receives an *a* or *b* rating in step 3, rate your relationship with that person on a scale of 1 (weak) to 5 (strong).

6. List any personal information that you are aware of, paying particular attention to significant dates such as birthdays and anniversaries. These dates give you an opportunity to maintain contact either through a telephone call or a card.

7. Think of things you can do to enhance the relationship. Remember to keep it timely, simple, and inexpensive. These can include social and professional events, telephone calls, and luncheon engagements.

8. Set aside a specified amount of time each week for implementation of your action plan, during which you devote your attention to relationship development. Invitations to business events and seminars you are already planning to attend can be included, and they have the benefit of not costing you additional time and effort.

9. Identify your ten most desirable contacts, and make a special effort to cultivate a positive relationship with them.

10. Periodically update your card file and formulate fresh ideas for making contacts.

Expansion of Your Referral Base

The final step in creating and maintaining a client referral system is to expand your existing referral base. In order to help you do so, I have developed six action steps. In addition to identifying each of these steps, I have outlined criteria for evaluating your present situation and actions you can take to upgrade when possible.

Step One: Identify Key clients who have made referrals in the past but no longer do so. Once you have identified these clients, you should try to determine possible reasons for the cessation of the referrals. Such reasons might include:

- We haven't asked them to refer lately.
- We didn't fulfill their expectations about the way they thought we would handle the latest referral to us.
- We haven't made them aware of the benefits we have provided to the people they referred to us.
- We might not be in their "circle of contacts" anymore.
- We never thanked them for previous referrals or sent a tangible token of our appreciation.
- We gave the referral a break in price, but not the client making the referral.

After examining the situation, contact the client and attempt to get him to make referrals again.

The following actions can be used to aid you in making the request.

- Make amends if you erred.
- Tell the client that she is a key client, and you are looking for more like her in the industry.
- Beef up value-added services on her engagement.
- Refer new business to her.
- Put "mountain climbers" on her engagement.
- Make her aware of the services that you are providing.

Step Two: Identify clients who regularly make referrals and take action to maintain that relationship. Relevant actions include:

- Thanking them by personal note.
- Sending them referrals when appropriate.
- Sending information they may be interested in.
- Performing value-added services for clients that make referrals.
- Introducing them to other people in your network.
- Saying "thank you" in person or by telephone.
- Informing them of positive results derived from referrals they made.

- Asking if you can use their names as referral sources.

Step Three: Identify "A" clients who should make referrals but do not, and initiate actions to get them to make referrals. Relevant actions include:

- Determining the possible cause for their failure to make referrals.
- Developing more personal relationships in their organization.
- Educating them about your need for referrals.
- Making referrals on their behalf.

Step Four: Introduce the idea of obtaining client referrals from satisfied clients in early contacts with new clients. Relevant actions include the following:

- In your first meeting with a new client, explain that your goals include doing a good job that will encourage him to (1) talk to his friends about you, (2) refer you, and (3) help you expand your area of expertise through contacts in the industry.
- Stress that "word-of-mouth" is your major marketing tool.
- At the end of your initial engagement, reaffirm the value of your services.
- Ask the client if he knows of any ways in which you can expand your client base.

Step Five: Conduct satisfaction meetings during which you seek referrals. In this meeting, specific actions for planting the seed and soliciting referrals include:

- Indicating to the client that you value him, and mentioning that you have the resources to take on new clients.

- Requesting the client's permission to use him as a reference.

- Asking for any details about how you might have exceeded the client's expectations, and requesting permission to refer to these in discussions with potential clients.

Step Six: Work with sporadic client referral sources, trying to get them to make referrals more frequently. Relevant actions include:

- Reporting to them on the outcome of previous referrals.

- If you failed to take an engagement from a referral source, explaining why and thanking them for the effort.

- Educating them about other types of work that you do.

- Increasing your frequency of communication with them.

By putting this system into practice and initiating the recommended action steps, you will find that your referral base will grow to become a consistent source of revenue enhancement. One of the major reasons for a small referral base is among those most obvious and simple: People are afraid to ask for them. In today's competitive environment this is a trap you must not allow yourself to fall into. Referrals are an integral part of your marketing operation, and if you use the system described in this chapter, they can be solicited in a way that allows you to operate inside your comfort zone.

10

Improving Your Billing and Collection Results

One of the most persistent problems encountered by service professionals is an inefficient billing and collection system that results in a failure to obtain revenues that can and should be collected. Instead, many service professionals settle for less than they are entitled to. The purpose of this chapter is to identify common inefficiencies and explain how they can be corrected. I will introduce four cardinal rules that must be consciously considered on a recurring basis in order to obtain the full amount of revenue to which you are entitled.

COMMON INEFFICIENCIES

In my consulting practice I have encountered four common inefficiencies that crop up at one time or another in virtually all service firms. They are under-bidding up front, poor record keeping, scope changes, and poor staffing assignments. Each of these inefficiencies will be discussed in turn.

Underbidding Up Front

The most common cause of underbidding an engagement is that the service provider does not know what it will cost to complete the job. All too often a bid is tendered due to competitive pricing considerations rather than as the result of a realistic assessment of the costs that will be incurred during the engagement. Typically, there is little or no pre-engagement planning prior to the submission of the bid.

Sloppy Record Keeping

Too many professional service providers do not keep track of the actual time they invest in the engagement. This includes time invested in incidental consulting over the telephone, document reviews, and fielding questions from client personnel or advisors. The result is that numerous potentially billable hours that are invested in the engagement are not accounted for. The service provider is often sidetracked from the task at hand by client-induced inquiries, but fails to include this time in invoice statements. Software is now available to keep track of phone calls.

Scope Changes

Once an engagement has begun, it is not uncommon for the client to expect that additional "small" problems will be taken care of under the terms of the original agreement. When this happens, service providers will frequently consent to scope changes without billing for them. The service professional may do so because he wants to be "a nice guy" or because he fears rejection on a future engagement bid.

Poor Assignment Staffing

One of the great wastes encountered by professional service providers is that partners and managers with high billing rates find themselves doing work that should have been done by lower-level technical or support staff. They do so because the work was done incorrectly or because they feel a need to be in control of all aspects of the engagement. Many of these partner hours are either not invoiced or need to be discounted. This results in an unnecessary loss of revenue.

As a result of the inefficiencies just discussed, service providers can find themselves caught in a terrible trap. You may find yourself working harder and harder to make the bottom line. Quite often, gross revenue will be high because your prices are competitive, but you are working harder to maintain a reasonable level of net income because your margins are shrinking.

When you are caught in this trap, there is a psychological tendency to blame the client and resent him. In effect, you make the client "wrong" for being right about hiring you at a reduced fee or for taking advantage of scope changes to which you do not object. This destroys all of the elements of a horizontal relationship and often leads to a dissolving of the relationship.

Additionally, service professionals find themselves facing problems of burn-out and lower morale. This can lead to unnecessarily high staff turnover and all of the problems and costs associated with hiring new personnel.

THE FOUR CARDINAL RULES

To protect against these problems, I have developed four cardinal rules that help to ensure that you get all of the revenue to which you are entitled and to eliminate job performance inefficiencies. Each will be examined in turn.

Rule Number One: *Log, invoice, and collect all the legitimate costs involved in producing the results agreed to in the engagement letter.* Too many service providers do not keep adequate track of their time. Many will sit down at the end of the week and try to allocate billable hours according to criteria that are not always an accurate reflection of the hours they worked on the engagements. These criteria can include the expectations of firm management, the nature of the client fee agreement, the amount of billable time needed to meet expenses, and what the service provider thinks the client will be willing to pay. In short, the tendency is to reduce billing to an attitude or feeling, rather than a process.

To combat this tendency it is imperative to keep track of all chargeable and nonchargeable hours on a daily basis. Exhibit 10-1 provides a Daily Time Sheet designed by Jack Norman, the National Director of Taxation at the accounting firm of Pannell, Kerr & Forster. The form is divided into 15-minute increments, which allow you to keep track of your time as your working day progresses. Simply write the name of the client you are working for in the slots provided. This

Exhibit 10-1. Daily Timesheet Analysis.

<u>Wednesday</u>
Day of Week

<u>September</u> 28
Date

DAILY TIME SHEET ANALYSIS
(Schedule in Pencil, Actual in Ink)

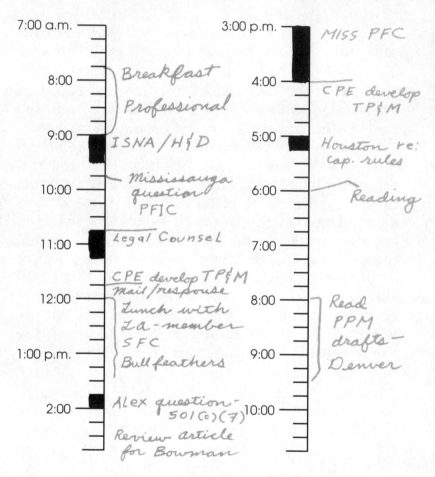

7:00 a.m.

8:00 — Breakfast
Professional

9:00 — ISNA / H&D

— Mississauga
10:00 — question
PFIC

11:00 — Legal Counsel

CPE develop TP&M
mail/response
12:00 — Lunch with
La-member
SFC
1:00 p.m. — Bull feathers

2:00 — Alex question-
501(c)(7)
Review article
for Bowman

3:00 p.m. — MISS PFC

4:00 — CPE develop
TP&M

5:00 — Houston re:
cap. rules

6:00 — Reading

7:00

8:00 — Read
PPM
drafts—
9:00 — Denver

10:00

Productivity: Percentage Chargeable <u>23%</u>

Total Nonchargeable <u>9.00</u>

Total Accounting <u>11.75</u>

record should include phone calls received from clients and any informal consultations in which you engage. At the end of the day, you total up your chargeable and nonchargeable hours and compute your percentage of billable time. Done on a daily basis, this allows you to maintain a permanent record of your time and takes much of the guesswork out of invoicing practices.

Your goal in initiating a timekeeping system is not only to maintain an accurate billing system, but also to keep track of how you and your staff are allocating your time. To determine any inefficiencies, make special note of time lost to poor planning, client-induced problems, and poor staff performance. Once these problems have been identified, you should take the steps necessary to correct them.

Rule Number Two: *Bill for all client-initiated changes to the original agreement and for all client-induced inefficiencies.* Prior to beginning work on a project you should draw up an engagement letter that clearly sets forth the nature and scope of the work to be done, a description of the deliverables, the hardcopy items to be produced, and all relevant timing and financial considerations. The engagement letter need not be overly legalistic, but should cover the basics of who, what, where, when, and how much. These are the terms that guide both parties in conducting the engagement.

In your initial engagement, don't start out by being an easy mark. Attempt to resell all scope

changes. If you do this tactfully and profession-
ally, you will not encounter the wrath of the
client. At the first sign of a scope change, simply say, "You are right to be concerned about
this. It's an important problem that needs to be
handled. I can take care of it for you in one of two
ways. I can finish the current project, and then
get back to you with the budget for the additional
work. Or we can cut another contract right now,
and do both projects simultaneously. Which is
best for you?"

After having said this, stop talking. You have
made it clear that you are not going to take on a
scope change without receiving additional compensation, and it is up to the client to respond. If
she asks you to include the scope change in the
original fee, tell her that cannot be done. You can
do so by saying: "I appreciate your wanting this
to be included in the original fee, but we have
a firm policy of billing tightly. We do not build
slack into our bids to cover for additional needs.
To try to do so would undermine the effective-
ness of our work on the current project, which
would not be good for either one of us." Once
again, stop talking as soon as you've made your
point, and let the client respond.

You can use a similar approach to bill for additional costs that are incurred as a consequence
of client inefficiencies. If you are losing a lot
of time to interruptions brought on by client
queries regarding other matters, or if the client
fails to provide you with materials necessary to

conduct the engagement, bring this to the attention of the client and attempt to bill for those hours. If you anticipate problems, this billing can be included in a separate invoice that provides an explanation of the additional work done.

Rule Number Three: *Remove discount pricing for C clients deemed to have the potential for upgrading in a way that maintains the primary firm-client relationship.* C clients are often created in two ways: (1) during new business discussions, billing and invoice expectations are not covered, or not covered fully; and (2) during engagements, scope changes are permitted or some discount pricing is engaged in. A mindset may be established in the client that these practices are routine on your part. This assumption is validated when the client takes advantage by adding scope changes or requesting discounts that go unchallenged.

The best way to upgrade C clients is to deal with the problem in a straightforward business discussion, during which you lay out the nature of the problem and propose a solution. Prior to such a meeting it is important for you to take some time to get your facts in order. You should be able to identify the specific jobs on which discounts were given or requested, and when scope changes occurred without an increase in compensation.

It is helpful to compute how much the firm has invested in serving the client. This computation will include a full account of the total hours devoted to client engagements, and will identify nonbillable hours, discounted hours, and freebies that have accrued, as well as out-of-pocket costs that have been incurred. Compare this figure with the amount of revenue that has been collected from the client. The difference between the two figures is *your* value gap. It is the gap that must be closed.

In meeting with your client, you can introduce the subject by saying, "I have been reviewing your file, and I want to bring something to your attention." Then show the figures and explain how the fees received have not matched the costs involved in doing the work. The gap has gone beyond the firm's policy, and you are bringing this up so it can be handled in a mutually beneficial manner.

Frequently, the client will be unaware of the nature of the problem encountered at your end, and will take some steps to upgrade the relationship. However, other clients will refuse to move to a higher plane, and say, "No deal." If this happens, you can do one of three things:

1. Ask him why, and listen to his explanations. Then reiterate why it is necessary for you to close the value gap.

2. Tell the client that you'll have to think about any future business dealings and let him contemplate the situation.

3. Tell the client that the decision is beyond your range of authority, that firm policy simply dictates that the gap must be closed.

In each of these responses you are giving the client an opportunity to reconsider his decision not to upgrade the relationship. If he values your services, there's a good chance that he will come back with a new offer in a reasonably short time frame. But if he continues to refuse to consider making changes in the fee structure, then you should consider dropping him from your service practice.

Keep in mind that being a C client is not always the fault of the client. C clients are frequently created by a professional service provider who lets the financial situation get out of the acceptable range. You can reassert control only by making the client aware of the situation and by closing the value gap.

Rule Number Four: *Look for opportunities for partners and managers to deliver value-added hours by pushing work down to the lowest level possible.* One of the great inefficiencies in service practices is to have high-level staff doing work that should be done at a lower level. Whenever this happens, the partner is working out of function. Frequently, these hours need to be discounted or go unbilled. The result is that you find yourself working harder to bring in less revenue.

To prevent this from happening, your pre-engagement planning should identify the work that is to be done by technical and support staff. If that work is not done properly, it should be corrected at that level and should not be allowed to bounce up to a partner who could be spending her time more productively on a task for which she can bill at her normal rate.

If the inefficiency is induced by the clients' support staff or technical staff not performing up to par, this fact should be brought to the client's attention. Any additional hours you are forced to work because of these inefficiencies can then be billed to the client, along with an explanation of the extra work involved.

LEARN FROM EVERY ENGAGEMENT

All the inefficiencies identified earlier in the chapter will occur to some degree in every service practice. Your goal is not to eliminate them, but to minimize and control them to the fullest extent possible. In doing so, you should strive to learn from every engagement. This will allow you to leverage your time in future engagements and minimize the inefficiencies that plague all service professionals.

The best way to learn from your engagements is to initiate a standard policy that requires all personnel to submit accurate timesheets. In those cases where you underbid on a job, and need to offer discounts to come in on budget, log the time even if you don't bill it. This information will be of importance to you for future engagements, and for submitting bids to clients in need of a similar service. By constantly keeping track of your hours and your bids, you will learn prudent bidding.

Secondly, you should examine the cause of all the unproductive time you become aware of. Unproductive time usually results from one of the following causes.

- Scope changes.
- Client requests and interruptions.
- Unsatisfactory work by client support staff.
- Unsatisfactory work by firm's support staff.
- Personality conflicts and breakdowns in communication.
- Technological inefficiencies.
- Partner working out of function.
- Unscheduled reworking of an acceptable project due to client-inspired changes.

Once the cause of unproductive time is isolated, you can take steps to correct the inefficiency. Too often, service providers fail to examine the nature of their billing practice as they attempt to look at the big picture and learn from it, so the inefficiencies continue unabated.

By applying the principles enunciated in this chapter, to implement a policy that permits an analysis of billing procedures and job productivity, you will create a learning procedure that helps you to maximize organizational efficiency and bring in additional revenue without a corresponding expansion in the number of engagements you take on.

11

Client Retention Planning

I wish I did not have to include this chapter. The intent of this book is to create smoothly operating, efficient systems that eliminate situations that threaten client–firm relationships. But we live in an imperfect world that cannot always be controlled. Business relationships undergo change for a variety of reasons, some of them directly attributable to you, and others beyond the scope of your area of responsibility.

In dealing with Mega clients, a light dose of paranoia is a good thing. The purposes of this chapter are to show how you can be alert to early warning signals that indicate trouble is on the horizon, and to provide a program for addressing these problems and retaining clients once the primary relationship has become threatened.

EARLY WARNING SIGNALS

Your existing clients are an essential resource that must be nurtured and protected. But your best clients are probably on the targeted hit list of other firms, and changes in personnel can also lead to a decision to replace your firm or to establish relationships with other professionals. This is particularly true in the present business environment where corporate mergers and buyouts have become commonplace and corporate executives have experienced a higher rate of turnover than at any time in our nation's history.

Losing a valued client is a painful experience that can be disadvantageous to both parties, yet few professional service firms have programs in place for dealing with events and potential problems that threaten business relationships. Invariably, the circumstances that lead to the dissolution of a valued relationship do not arise full-blown, and they can usually be seen in advance. The problem is that service providers are frequently blind to early warning signals and consequently fail to take the steps necessary to retain the client.

I have developed a list of early warning signals that commonly indicate that trouble of one sort or another is a-brewin'.

EARLY WARNING SIGNS

1. Failure to return phone calls.
2. Complaints about minor items.
3. Lack of response from key people.
4. Loss of contact with top management.
5. Fee resistance.
6. Slow payment of invoices.
7. A drying up of referrals.
8. Requests for changes in staffing the engagement.
9. Turnover in executive positions.
10. Solicitation of bids from the competition.
11. Requests for scope changes without fee increases.
12. Unrealistic demands.

Let's discuss each of these warning signals so you will have a foundation to work from in dealing with them. As we proceed, keep in mind that one or two of these signals do not mean a client is in danger, but together they will give you an early alert system.

Failure to Return Your Phone Calls

If your client has been responsive to your phone calls, but then becomes difficult to get in touch with or simply does not return your calls, use this as a strong indicator of possible problems. To make contact and resolve the situation, you can either call the person at night or get over to see him in person.

In my own practice I have not always been as sensitive to this warning signal as I might have been. As an example, I have one horror story to report that could probably have been minimized had I been more alert. In recent years I have developed a new niche, providing church growth and development services to ministries in the New Thought movement. Over the past two years I developed a close client/friend relationship with a minister in another state.

During a recent strategic planning workshop, I noticed that he seemed unusually stressed and brought this to his attention. He dismissed this as being "business as usual" pressure. As part of our friendship we often engaged in light-hearted, teasing banter, but in this instance my barbs were not laughed at, but apparently hit home and hurt.

In making my customary follow-up phone call to assess the client's perception of the planning session, I could not get through to him. After several additional calls, I asked the secretary if something was going on that I should know about. She dodged my question and told me she'd have him call me. I quit trying to get through, and about six weeks later I received a copy of a scathing letter addressed to my key client contact, the executive director of an association of New Thought Churches, in which this minister vented his anger. Eleven months after the incident, we finally had the opportunity to discuss the situation and begin healing the relationship.

The lesson to be learned? When in doubt check it out by doing whatever is necessary to gain certainty in the situation. If I had moved more quickly to open lines of communication, then the problem might not have had time to fester. But by proceeding in a "business as usual" style in spite of the early warning signal, I failed to address the problem of hurt feelings at a time when a few kind words and an apology were needed.

Complaints about Minor Items

I have a few clients who will sometimes complain about minor items, but there is nothing unusual about this. However, if you find a sudden shift in attitude, so that there is a litany of complaints, then you need to move quickly.

During my research for this chapter, a client gave me a wonderful example of how minor complaints can evolve into a major problem. Her prime client was hard of hearing. My client's usual receptionist was a woman with a deep, well-modulated voice, and she was away on an extended vacation. The temporary receptionist who replaced her had a grating, squeaky voice, which the client had a hard time understanding. The client complained about this a couple of times, and the server, knowing that the regular receptionist would return, did not go into a lengthy explanation of where the receptionist was, but simply thanked the client for bringing the problem to her attention. The hearing-impaired person, enraged over constantly having to ask "What did you say?" every time she called, finally gave the server an ultimatum, saying "Either the receptionist goes, or I go. Take your pick."

One of my early mentors once told me, "Dick, your clients will love you or loathe you for the strangest and smallest of reasons." In dealing with small problems and minor complaints, you must be sensitive to this fact. Had this server taken a few minutes to explain why the regular receptionist was not in the office and when she would return, the problem would have remained small. But because she dismissed the complaint as trivial and got on to "more important" business, the client was angered by a seeming lack of sensitivity.

Lack of Timely and Positive Response from Key People

This generally shows up as a consequence of a lack of enthusiasm for the recommended next steps that involve the additional use of your services. The surest way out of this thicket is to go straight to the client executive and ask, "Am I on target here? From my reading of your reaction I might have missed the mark and some changes might be necessary."

Loss of Contact with Key Management

During the early stages of the client–firm relationship, the server often has ready contact with members of the client's decision-making team. The amount of access will often shrink after the initial engagement, perhaps because the engagement team has delivered the goods but maybe because executives do not feel that the results have been adequate and have decided to place limits on the amount of additional work to be done or to end the relationship. This situation cannot be left to chance. The server needs to conduct end-of-engagement Client Satisfaction Meetings and, if necessary, between-engagement meetings to maintain contact. If diminishing contact is a problem, you should address it in the Client Satisfaction Meetings.

Fee Resistance

This usually shows up in the form of outright complaints about the ever growing costs of doing business. My accounting firm clients are often plagued by this warning signal. Many of their clients must have an audit. The costs to the accounting firm of providing the service increase every year, and these costs are passed on to the client. Some clients reach their "financial flinch point" and resistance sets in. If the problem is not surfaced and resolved, the accounting firm may find itself replaced by another firm.

Slow Payment of Invoices

This warning signal must be looked at and handled quickly. The slow payment can indicate dissatisfaction with an engagement or the client–firm relationship, a worsening financial situation, or all of the above. Your firm's policy should be to state at the beginning of the client-firm relationship, "It is our practice to invoice as the engagement proceeds, and we expect payment in full within 30–45 days upon invoice receipt. Do you anticipate any difficulty with this?" Once this policy is established, it is simple for you follow up on delinquent invoices by referring to the policy in making your inquiry.

A Drying Up of Referrals

Because referrals are generated by highly satisfied and enthusiastic clients, any evidence that a client is slowing down or discontinuing the provision of referrals must be looked at immediately. A consulting engineer client of mine experienced a loss of new business when a key client decided to stop sending him referrals. The client, an executive director of an association of land developers, felt that the engineer wasn't appreciative of the large number of leads he had given, so he developed a network of servers who were more responsive and thankful for the favors done. Saying thanks, and occasionally providing a nice dinner for the client, can go a long, long way in protecting your referral base. Once again, seemingly minor responses can make a big difference.

Requests for Changes in Staffing the Engagement

Some servers develop a hard and fast position when faced with this situation. They tend to feel that staffing the engagement is their prerogative, not the client's. Fortunately, this attitude is changing rapidly. The key to handling this problem is to attempt to get all the facts on the table and to get specific reasons from the client as to the real reason she wants the person changed. If the request is genuine and the client truly believes the employee is a detriment to the relationship, the next step is to make the change if you have a qualified replacement. This can be difficult if you do not have a qualified replacement, or if the person who could fill in is not available due to other commitments. In the former case you are faced with the daunting problem of asking the client to back down, which carries with it the chance of losing the engagement or even the relationship. In the latter case, you may be able to put a portion of the job on temporary hold until the qualified replacement becomes available. In either case, the original staff person must be made aware of the situation and given the facts as told to you. Failure to be candid tends to disempower the staff person, and potentially correctable problems go unresolved.

Turnover in Executive Positions in the Client Organization

The client–firm relationship is made up of one or more relationships with members of the client decision-making team for the use of services you provide. Should you encounter turnover in executive positions, you must arrange to meet the replacements and make them aware of the benefits your firm is providing. Quite often, the new executives have their own favorite service providers, and they are looking for the opportunity to bring them in.

Solicitation of Bids from the Competition

The worst scenario is to learn about a competitive bid after the fact. Less painful, yet still dangerous, is to have your client tell you that he is going to seek bids from firms you compete with. I've learned to confront this situation head-on by asking my client, "Would you mind telling me why the decision has been made to reach beyond the relationship we have established? Is there a problem that we need to talk about?"

Requests for Scope Changes

This is a frequent and potentially costly predicament. A well-written letter of agreement is your most helpful tool in forestalling such requests. I learned long ago to honor these requests as important, and to suggest that I draft a supplemental letter of agreement to cover the agreed-on scope change. I generally do so by saying, "Ms. Client, your request is sound and is something we should deal with. As soon as we complete this portion of the work, I'll be glad to send you a draft of the additional fees involved in producing the results you want and deserve." If the client persists in wanting the scope change without an increase in fees, I say, "I agree that this is important to you. Because it is important to you, it is important to me to do the best job I can. This will involve additional time and personnel to produce the desired results." This lets the client know that you are incurring additional costs to undertake the scope change, and that it is unfair to expect you to absorb those costs without recompense.

Unrealistic Demands

This usually occurs during the negotiations for the initial engagement. The client wants the moon and is willing to pay only for a small shop in Newark. The answer? Honor the demand and convert the unrealistic aspect of it into a long-range goal that the client might one day hope to achieve through the efficient use of your resources. I've frequently heard myself saying, "Mr. Client, I appreciate that you would like to have every member of your staff bring in new business. That is a goal we can work toward. In the meantime, let's focus on improving the marketing skills of the people who are attending my Getting New Clients workshop." This brings short-term expectations down to a manageable level, without sacrificing the client's long-term goals and dreams.

IDENTIFYING VULNERABLE SITUATIONS

When early warning signals such as those listed above first begin to appear, the tendency is to ignore them and hope they will go away. Unfortunately, this rarely happens. In order to address small problems before they become major problems, it is necessary to be alert to these early tip-offs and then take action on them immediately.

Client retention planning can best be viewed as an extension of client service planning. Just as it is important to plan for an engagement by taking note of the situation from the client's side of the desk, it is also important to evaluate the services you have provided from the client's perspective.

Every business relationship has potential vulnerabilities, and these vulnerabilities can be monitored on a regular basis. Even though your goal is always to provide quality service, breakdowns can occur. Exhibit 11-1 provides a policy statement and checklist that permits you to monitor potential vulnerablities with existing clients and to remain alert to early warning signals that threaten the relationship. This checklist should be completed by relevant personnel at the end of every engagement, and appropriate action should be undertaken to protect the relationship whenever warning signs appear.

Exhibit 11-1. Vulnerable situations.

In every relationship there is a vulnerability for things to go sour. In a service environment vulnerable situations will always arise when service is substandard. Our whole organization aims at providing quality service, but in certain situations there may still

Exhibit 11-1. Continued.

be vulnerability. If the response to any of the following questions is positive, look at the impact it may have. Most deal with recent events that have occurred in the last twelve months.

1. Have we been late in meeting our commitments?

2. Have we put new personnel on the engagement team?

3. Have we had to replace any of the team members to satisfy the client?

4. Have we given bad advice that has cost the client money?

5. Have we taken key members of the client service team off the account?

6. Have any key members of the client service team left the firm?

7. Have we disagreed with the client on important issues?

8. Has the client appointed a new chief executive?

9. Has a new key board member been appointed?

10. Does the CEO have a close relationship with an individual in another competitive firm?

11. Is the client served by a bank or an attorney who does not respect us as a quality firm?

12. Have we not had regular monthly contact with the client?

13. Have we received limited or no calls for consultation?

14. Is the company in financial trouble?

15. Is there dissatisfaction on the client's part with our industry knowledge?

16. Have we surprised the client lately with a significant issue?

17. Have we reversed a position on advice given previously?

18. Is the personal chemistry between any key member of the client service team and client management a problem?

19. Is there a political situation brewing in the client organization?

20. Do we have limited relationships?

21. Are there effectively no relationships between the partner and client?

22. Does the client have a history of rotating service providers?

23. Has the client acquired a company or business served by another firm that offers similar services?

24. Is the client's parent company served by others who compete with us?

25. Has the client been recently acquired by a company with other service providers?

26. Is the client vulnerable to takeover?

EVALUATING THE SITUATION

Once potential problem areas that threaten the primary client–firm relationship have appeared, the first step required for addressing them is to undertake a careful analysis of the situation. The *source* of the problem needs to be located and uncovered.

In our discussion of the Client Service Plan in Chapter 6, we looked at the network of relationships that hold the firm and the client together (see Exhibit 11-2). As soon as retention planning needs to be activated, you should examine the network of relationships to determine where the stress points are. You must ask yourself questions such as: What are the pivotal relationships on project X? At what point has the dissatisfaction been expressed? Are personality conflicts involved? Have there been problems with either the quality or the delivery of the product? Evaluating the answers to such questions will allow you to focus attention on the pertinent problem.

Secondly, an informal meeting with the client is often necessary to obtain a full understanding of the problem. In this meeting the following four action steps are recommended.

1. Meet face-to-face to allow and encourage the client to express himself completely and unburden all of his thoughts and feelings about the situation to you—a concerned, receptive listener.

Exhibit 11-2. Network of relationships.

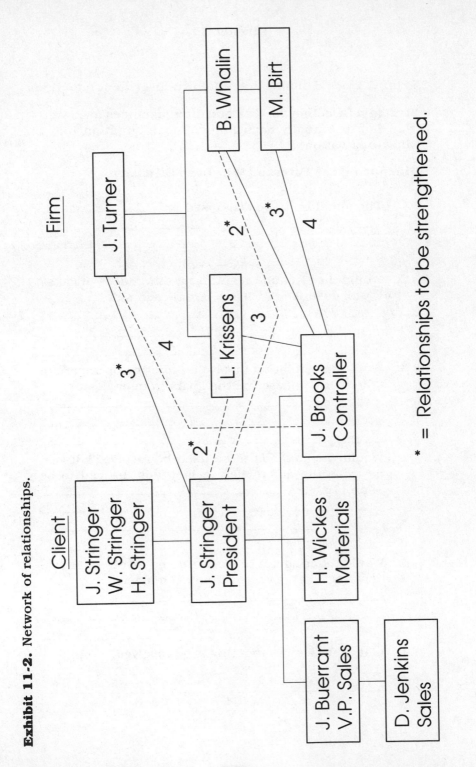

Client

Firm

J. Stringer
W. Stringer
H. Stringer

J. Stringer
President

H. Wickes
Materials

J. Buerrant
V.P. Sales

D. Jenkins
Sales

J. Turner

L. Krissens

J. Brooks
Controller

B. Whalin

M. Birt

3*

4

2*

3

2*

3

2*

3*

4

* = Relationships to be strengthened.

Exhibit 11-3 Handling potential win-lose client situations

Strategy: Selecting the time and circumstances to convert what is a potentially damaging win-lose situation into a win-win situation.

Diagnosing the Potential Win-Lose Situation

1. The situation to be diagnosed is _____
   _____
   _____
   _____

2. Would the situation result from differences of facts? If yes, describe the "facts" from each side. _____
   _____
   _____
   _____

3. Would the situation involve conflicting or uncertain *goals*? If yes, describe the goals from each side.
   _____
   _____
   _____

4. Would the *methods* to be used be involved? If yes, describe the differences in methods deemed to be appropriate. _____ _____
   _____
   _____
   _____

5. Would differing notions of *value* be involved? If yes, describe what is valued from each side. _____
   _____
   _____
   _____

6. List other factors that might be involved. _____
   _____
   _____
   _____

2. Gently probe to determine if there are any *hidden* problems besides the ones expressed by the client. If present, these factors usually are the main problem. You might ask, "In addition to what you just told me, are there any other things I should know about?"

3. Even if you are told off in strong language, recognize that much of the anger is not directed at you personally. You just happen to be in the line of fire.

4. Any response you do make should be on a high plane. A professional cannot have too many friends or too few enemies. Don't engage in verbal sparring matches.

After you have obtained the relevant information, the final step involved in evaluating the problem is to write up a clear, concise diagnosis. Exhibit 11-3 provides a form designed for use as a diagnostic tool. When completed, it will give you a full description of the nature and scope of your problem.

TAKING CORRECTIVE ACTION

Once the problem has been identified, the next step is to undertake the necessary corrective action. This might include a change in the use of resources, a change in personnel, or more intensive training.

Above all, let the client know that you are aware that the problem exists and that you are concerned about solving it.

LONG-TERM CLIENT RETENTION PLANNING

To be successful, client retention planning should not be relegated to crisis situations and known problem areas, but should be an integral part of your client service planning for Mega, Key, and "A" clients. This can be done in a five-step process.

Step One. For each client identified, develop sufficient client-centered data on the client's organization, markets and competition, industry trends, needs, and services provided. In undertaking this analysis, you should be able to answer the following questions:

- What is the status of the client's industry?
- What are the major success factors within the industry?
- What are the client's major business goals?
- What are the client's major business values?
- Does the client have a formalized program for goal setting?
- How have our services addressed the client's goals and values?

Step Two. Estimate the degree of client satisfaction with your present service offerings. Identify current and potential problems in working with each client. The relevant questions for analysis include the following.

- How did we obtain the engagement?
- In our previous engagements, what made the client happy?
- In our previous engagements, what made the client unhappy?
- Have we had any significant problems in serving the client? If so, identify them.
- What does the client see as our firm's greatest strength?
- What does the client see as our firm's greatest weakness?
- How does the client define our firm's role?
- What benefits has the client realized as a result of our services?

Step Three. Assess the quality of the relationships between members of your client's organization and your firm. Relevant questions include:

- Who are the major decision makers in the client's organization?
- Are they influenced by other key individuals?
- What values and goals are important to them?
- What do they think of our firm?

- Have they ever expressed dissatisfaction with any of our client personnel?

- In examining dual organization charts, do members of our engagement team appear to be on good relations with client personnel?

- Have we done anything the major decision makers regard as a beneficial "extra" service?

Step Four. Identify and evaluate the nature of the total communications between the client and your firm, including an assessment of the information available in Client Alert Reports and an evalution of Client Satisfaction Meetings. Relevant questions include:

- What are the client's major business problems?

- Why has the client been unable to make progress on a particular business goal?

- Have we discussed these areas with key client personnel?

- What has the client done to correct the problem?

- What have we done to help the client correct the problem? Does she see this as a beneficial service?

- Are there any problems of which the client is not aware that we consider serious?

- What have we done to bring these problems to her attention?

Step Five. For each client develop a client retention plan that integrates the data collected in steps one through four. This plan should develop action priorities and assign specific responsibilities to prevent or correct any client dissatisfactions, thus minimizing the possibility of your firm's being replaced. Relevant questions include:

- What one or two things could we accomplish in the coming year that the client would see as an improved service?

- Who is our primary competition for the client's work? How are they positioning themselves?

- In what areas must we build the depth of our client service team?

- How do we need to change the client's perception of our firm?

- What specific action steps will be assigned to initiate that change?

- How can we build better relations with key client decision makers?

As mentioned previously, the key to retaining your most valued clients is to establish client-centered relationships with them. Even though this involves a considerable investment on your part, it will pay huge dividends should the client be wooed by an aggressive firm or if unfortunate job performance problems arise during the course of an engagement.

To maintain that relationship it is important to have a smoothly functioning communication loop working at all levels. To aid in the achievement of this goal, Exhibits 11-4 through 11-6 describe the client retention responsibilities for staff, engagement managers, and partners. These responsibilites should be incorporated into the client retention plan developed in step five.

Exhibit 11-4. Client retention responsibilities for staff.

1. Service Improvement:
   a) Alert to areas for possible inclusion in management letter and bringing these items to senior's attention.
   b) Respond timely and accurately on assignments.
   c) Maintain good relationship with client's personnel.
   d) Maintain and improve his technical ability.
   e) Improve understanding of client's system and operations.
   Satisfaction:
   Securing client's feedback re satisfaction not handled by staff.
2. Communication During Engagement:
   a) Develop a relationship with client personnel to foster exchange of information.

b) Maintain professional bearing.

Between engagements:

None unless specifically assigned.

3. Understanding Key Clients

Executives – none at this level

Business:

Maintain an awareness of nature of the business and develop an understanding of the business.

Industry:

Read literature related to the industry.

Exhibit 11-5. Client retention responsibilities for engagement managers.

Service

1. Review scope of engagement.

2. Review results of prior program, working papers, management letters, etc.

3. Schedule and conduct pre-engagement planning session.

4. Supervise and review the progress of engagement for accuracy and complexities.

5. Ensure the timely completion of engagement.

Exhibit 11-5. Continued.

6. Review the drafting of the management letter or final report.

Communication

1. Conduct periodic interviews with client to review progress and identify any problems.

2. Make periodic checks between engagement client contact to maintain visibility and demonstrate interest on the part of the firm.

3. Establish the time frame of the engagement.

Understanding of Key Client

1. Obtain a list of key personnel executives.

2. Obtain a knowledge of the client industry and the client's place in the industry.

3. Instigate discussion with partner and other knowledgeable people regarding key client personnel.

4. Remain current with client industry periodicals and key indicators.

5. Be familiar with industry terminology.

6. Establish, to the extent possible, personal relationships with key client executive personnel.

7. Conduct interview with key client executives to identify their, and the business's, goals and expectations.

Relationships

1. Identify and establish relationships with "comers" in the client firm.

2. Develop an awareness of when it is appropriate to get someone else involved.

Exhibit 11-6. Client retention responsibilities for partner.

1. Service:

   Improvement and satisfaction:

   > Determine that adequate consideration is given to service improvement and client satisfaction.

2. Communication:

   Plan and implement continuing communication with appropriate client personnel.

3. Understanding of Key Clients:

   Executives:

   > Determine that key executives' goals and expectations are recognized.

   Business:

   > Assume responsibility for an understanding of client business and industry.

Exhibit 11-6. Continued

> 4. Relationships:
>
> Plan and implement enhancement and establishment of strong relations.
>
> Determine and plan necessity of transfer of relationship to others.

MANAGING THE BAD NEWS

Everything we have been discussing in this book has been designed to prevent the loss of your primary client–firm relationships. But sometimes it happens. It might happen for reasons that you could not control, such as: a client is merged; there is a turnover in management; the client encounters hard times and the board dictates changes; or a closely held corporation goes out of business because of the death of the owner. Sometimes the termination is due to mistakes on your part, such as poor service or an upset that gets out of hand.

For whatever reason, getting fired is never fun. When it does occur, however, it is important to remember that the loss of the primary client-firm relationship is not necessarily automatic. If you act in a smart, sensitive manner, you may be able to retain a portion of your business, or you may create opportunities for reestablishing the relationship.

I mentioned earlier that I frequently serve in a mentor role, acting as director of marketing for firms that are just building their marketing programs. Once the program is underway, it is understood that the firm will hire a full-time marketing director. This means that my release is unavoidable, although the timing is frequently uncertain. I have discovered that if I build solid, supportive relationships within the firm, I am often asked to serve in certain specialized areas that the new person isn't proficient in. So even after the new director is brought in, I retain a portion of the work.

Termination of the service relationship frequently comes in a letter that accompanies the final installment on your invoice. In tactful language it says that the client enjoyed the long relationship, but that the completion of the current scope of the work brings your employment to a close. The worst thing that you can do at this point is to let this be the final chapter. Instead, a termination notice should activate a chain of analysis and planning that is designed to get you a face-to-face meeting with the person who has the power to rehire you.

The purpose of such a meeting is to determine if something was not done that was expected, or if something was done that was not up to expectations. In trying to set up the meeting, be sure to accept responsibility for the situation. You do not want to put off a client executive by making him feel like the bad guy. There is no room for name calling or finger pointing.

If the client executive does not want to see you, tell him that it is firm policy. Explain that you need to return certain materials to the client, and that you wish to make certain that all loose ends are wrapped up. Assure him that it won't take long to do so.

In the meeting, your strategy should be to ask questions and listen. Frequently, you will find that the formal reason for the termination is not the real reason. As an example, a national accounting firm once retained me to contact a growing number of dissatisfied clients it was losing to see if I could determine why business was being lost. One of these clients claimed that the reason for the termination of the accounting firm was a fee dispute. But sitting over lunch, the client executive responded to my probing questions by blurting out: "I know what you're after, and I sense that you can be trusted to get the story straight. It was bad enough when this bozo [one of the accounting firm's partners] started putting his hands all over a couple of the secretaries in my office. He had an annoying habit of trying to sell me more work, which I suppose comes with the territory. But the last straw was when we were sitting in my club, and the jerk put his cigar butt out in his grapefruit. I figured I didn't have to put up with that."

I was extremely sympathetic. A client should never have to put up with rude behavior. My response was to tell him so, and then to ask whether he would reconsider the decision to terminate the client–firm relationship if someone else in the accounting firm were assigned to handle the engagement. He said that he would think about it. I reported my findings to the accounting firm's managing partner, who immediately swung into action, and the rebuilding process began. The point is that an opportunity was there to save the relationship that no one knew about until the real reason for the termination had been brought to light.

Even when the relationship is severed, you should still send "I've been thinking of you" notes to the other decision makers in the organization that you have established quality relationships with. This can often lead to referrals or to new business if the executive moves to another firm or there are personnel changes in her present firm. For example, I was once fired from a consulting job as a consequence of a squabble with one of the firm's partners. After my termination, I maintained my relationship with the director of training by asking him to critique one of my early drafts for a book. When I got to his city on other business, I would call and see how he was doing. The key was to keep the relationship with one of my prime contacts open by looking for and capitalizing on opportunities to stay in his mind. I never asked for any additional business, but simply proved by my persistance that I valued the friendship and the relationship. Eventually, he saw to it that I was rehired after the other partner moved to another firm.

Getting fired is never fun, but every situation, no matter how bad, creates opportunities for you to practice the client-centered skills of listening, learning, and understanding. The best you can ever be expected to do when confronted with a bad situation is find a way to learn from it. Instead of reacting with anger and assessing blame, keep your act together. When possible, seek opportunities to maintain the relationship, or at least a reduced level of service. Even if one relationship goes sour inside a client organization, retain your relationships with other people in the organization. Keep track of promotions and personnel changes. New business derived from executives in former client organizations should be a goal of your marketing program, and it is frequently made possible by handling worst-case scenarios with grace, dignity, and class.

As an example, I have a good friend who was a consultant to a Big 8 accounting firm for several years. Then one day he was abruptly fired. The managing partner in the division he worked in had a serious alcohol problem and needed a scapegoat to cover up his own deteriorating performance. My friend was the most convenient scapegoat.

Instead of throwing a temper tantrum, and telling the managing partner exactly what he thought of him, my friend quickly realized that he could no longer work in that division as long as the managing partner remained entrenched as an executive officer in the firm. Very quietly, he spoke with the four other partners in the division about what had transpired, thanked them for their cooperation, and said that he was sorry the managing partner's drinking problem had gotten so far out of hand. By letting them know that he felt no personal animosity toward them, he kept future doors open. A short while later he received a phone call from one of the junior partners, who said he was leaving the Big 8 firm to take a job with a mid-size consulting firm. He had two projects that were waiting on his desk for his arrival, and he wanted to know whether my friend would be available to assist him on those projects. Two years have since passed, and my friend has established a much more lucrative and amiable relationship with this client than he ever had with the Big 8 firm. Although he didn't know it at the time, his getting fired simply opened a new door—a door that he had put himself in position to walk through.

12

Making Client-Centered Marketing Work for You

As I said in the Introduction, my goal in writing this book is to provide you with actionable information that empowers you to sense, sell, serve, and satisfy the needs of your desirable clients, and to provide you with a client-centered marketing system that you will never outgrow. The final point to be made in regard to this system is that the key to making it work for you is to incorporate the strategies and guidelines that form the core of the client-centered marketing approach into your regular business procedures. Successful marketing cannot be done on a haphazard business, but is an integral part of every engagement. This is true even if you are not conscious of it as you conduct the engagement.

My experience as a consultant and practitioner in the services profession has shown that when a client-centered marketing system is integrated into your standard way of doing business, your existing clients will become your private, proprietary market, your revenue will increase, and your clients will be better served.

Each of the preceding chapters in this book has described strategies and guidelines that are specifically related to a particular subject area. At the foundation of all of these strategies and guidelines is the belief that there is no substitute for honesty, integrity, commitment, and quality service.

As a means of providing a short-hand summary of the basic actions that guide the client-centered marketing approach, I have compiled a list of "Dos" and "Don'ts" that are applicable at all stages of the engagement. When put into practice, this system will ensure that your best marketing days are still ahead of you, and that your clients will receive the quality service they are seeking.

As a professional, *do*:

1. Dress in a manner that will help you put forth a professional and trustworthy appearance.

2. Maintain a positive attitude toward the client. Communicate your integrity and professional competence visibly in your attitude and behavior.

3. Establish empathy through the proper use of eye contact and good listening skills, such as periodically repeating the client's thoughts in order to confirm an accurate understanding.

4. Keep abreast of current events and developments in the client's organization.

5. Research and become informed about the client's industry and market.

6. Be aware of the client's problems and concerns.

7. Promptly return all client phone calls and inquiries.

8. Be prompt on deliveries and punctual for scheduled meetings and appointments.

As a professional, *don't*:

1. Create an unnecessary vertical relationship with the client.

2. Talk down to the client. Avoid any antago-
   nizing or patronizing comments.

3. Argue with the client in ways that hurt his
   self-esteem.

4. Break scheduled appointments or fail to
   return telephone calls.

5. Offend the client with personal habits. For
   example, do not smoke if he doesn't do so
   himself.

In providing your service, *do*:

1. Obtain a definition of the client's problems and needs. You should get this definition in her own words.

2. Take a visible interest in the problems of
   the client's business.

3. Communicate your expertise in a diplo-
   matic way.

4. Discuss the problem specifics with the
   client first, not with her employees.

5. Estimate the monetary and personal
   benefits of your service to the client, and
   make the client aware of those benefits.

6. Inform the client of the availability of
   other services you provide.

7. Protect the client's self-esteem. This is
   particularly essential when discussing

sensitive problem areas that may cause embarrassment to her.

8. Deliver your service on schedule.

9. Maintain regular contact by telephone or in face-to-face conversations.

10. Make certain that the client knows that you are working for her, and that your efforts are focused on her needs and problems.

11. Make your results visible.

12. Copy and mail relevant articles to the client.

13. Get involved in organizations that the client participates in, or share mutual interests with her.

14. Let the client know that you care about her as a person, not only as a business colleague.

In providing your service, *don't*:

1. Sell something you don't have or can't produce.

2. Sell your service too cheaply.

3. Ignore the client or take her for granted.

4. Let your ego get in the way of developing a horizontal relationship. You should not put the client down by making her feel inferior.

5. Make general recommendations or be too vague.

In representing your firm to the client, *do*:

1. Determine what the client wants and needs to know about your firm, then . . .
2. Be prepared to explain the totality of the firm's services in terms of client benefits.
3. Tell the client about your back-up personnel.
4. Educate the client as to the competency and reputation of your firm.
5. Make the client aware of your publications and put him on your mailing list.
6. Prepare effective management and engagement letters.
7. Make your analysis of raw data available to the client.
8. Let the client know about services your firm has performed for other clients.

In representing your firm to the client, *don't*:

1. Sell for size and size alone.
2. Set cost solely on the size of the engagement.
3. Promise more than the firm is prepared to deliver.
4. Agree to scope changes during the engagement just to be "nice."

In addressing client needs and problems, *do*:

1. Identify the problem and what is needed and being lost.

2. Determine the client's future needs.

3. Give the client the opportunity to surface his problems.

4. Appraise the client for reactions to the estimated fee.

5. Use tact and try to be as relaxed as possible.

6. Present your service as a benefit and an opportunity. Give examples of favorable outcomes, such as savings, control, information, and solutions.

7. Periodically review the client's position.

8. Offer constructive advice in the form of a good management letter.

In addressing client needs and problems, *don't*:

1. Ignore the client's perception of his problem.

2. Attempt to impose your views on him.

3. Tell the client that he is wrong. His self-esteem will be threatened. Don't make him feel inferior or stupid by lecturing him.

4. Begin by discussing cost.

5. Fault the client by assessing blame.

Appendix A

Using the SIC Code

The Standard Industrial Classification (SIC) system is the federal government's numerical coding system to provide a "standard industry" classification for every existing business in the United States. First developed in the 1940s, the SIC identifies manufacturing and nonmanufacturing industries for the purposes of data collection and reporting.

Within the system, each major area of activity, referred to as a division (A, B, C, etc.), is first assigned a range of two-digit classification codes. At present there are 12 major divisions. For example, the manufacturing division (division D) includes SICs 20 to 39. Each two-digit designation denotes a major group, such as SIC 20—Food. Each major group is subdivided into three-digit Industry Groups, such as SIC 208—beverages. At the next level of detail, 4-digit specific industries are identified (SIC 2082—malt beverages, or SIC 2086—bottled and canned soft drinks).

The SIC was developed for use in the classification of establishments by the type of activity in which they are engaged. An *establishment* is an economic unit, generally at a single physical location, where business is conducted or where services or industrial operations are performed. An establishment is not necessarily identical with an enterprise or company, which may consist of one or more establishments.

An establishment is assigned an industry code on the basis of its primary activity. A primary activity is determined by its principal product or group of products produced or distributed, or services rendered. The SIC classifies industry groups that are sufficiently broad to differentiate lines of business reasonably and meaningfully.

Developed initially for use within government for statistical purposes, the SIC is now widely used by service firms. The uses include

- Determining the current industry mix for the service's practice.
- Identifying emerging and rapidly growing industries.
- Zeroing in on the service's best prospects and avoiding non-prospects in order to make new business development more efficient.

The Office of Management and Budget (OMB) is responsible for the development of the SIC. The OMB publishes an official manual, *Standard Industrial Classification Manual*, available from the U. S. Government Printing Office (GPO), Washington, DC 20402.

The government's update schedule calls for revisions every ten years, but as with many government operations, the revision is behind schedule. In a statement dated February 14, 1986, the OMB announced some long overdue changes to be considered in updating the *Manual*. The OMB's Technical Committee on Industrial Classification (TCIC) will have the final word on whether any of the recommended changes will occur. In all, more than 1000 different changes have been proposed by outside users, with some 40 percent being accepted by the TCIC for consideration. The TCIC has recommended that 78 current industry titles be deleted through mergers with other industries and that 79 new industries be added to the system by subdividing or restructuring existing industries. A new two-digit major group (87) has been proposed for selected professional and technical services, made up from parts of current major groups 73 (Business Services) and 89 (Miscellaneous Services).

A copy of OMB's Federal Register notice, along with the complete list of TCIC recommendations, is available from the Office of Management and Budget, Washington, DC 20503.

SOME PROBLEMS

There are about 1000 four-digit SIC codes established by the government. But the existing SIC structure does not reflect the fundamental structural changes in American industry such as the growth of services, rapidly advancing technologies, and the decline of Rust Belt industries such as manufacturing and tool and die.

Another problem is that attempting to classify all businesses according to a code with just four digits falls well short of an adequate segmentation system. Actually, the current SIC system ignores marketing needs in the first place. As the government describes its purpose, SIC is "one of the most important tools that has been developed to promote the comparability of statistics describing various facets of the nation." In other words, the SIC is a convenience for the study of American industry. In effect, Uncle Sam is saying, "Want to use my system, fellows? You're welcome, but remember, it was designed for our use and not yours."

SOME INTERIM SOLUTIONS

Direct response list compilers have realized that various classifications can be more precisely defined by "Yellow Pages" directory categories. In many cases, list compilers have subdivided the four-digit numbers and used letters to designate subcategories. For example, existing code 5023 is defined as Home Furnishings. Thanks to the good work of the list compilers, this category is now subdivided as follows:

5023A   Carpet and floor covering

5023B   China and glassware

5023C   Curtain and drapery

USING RESOURCES AVAILABLE TO YOU

I seldom use the official government *Manual* anymore, given the sad state of affairs. Instead, I use the following sources of SIC data.

1. "Lists of 14 Million Businesses: compiled from the Yellow Pages," from American Business Lists, Inc., 5707 South 86th Circle, P.O. Box 27347, Omaha, NE 68127, mailed free on request. This directory is useful in identifying the primary four-digit SIC for an establishment, and for getting some sense of the total size of the industry. The first list in the catalog is listed in alphabetical order for ease in finding the code. For example, the current edition shows:

    8391   Accountants   113,842 [the number in the U. S.]

2. Burnette Mailing List Catalog, Ed Burnette Consultants, Inc., 99 West Sheffield Ave., Englewood, NJ 07631, 1-800-223-7777. After I get the primary SIC code, this list gives a better breakdown. For example, the American Business Lists, Inc., shows:

    7311   Advertising Agencies
           & Counsellors   23117

    Under 7311, the Burnette list shows:

    Advertising Agencies—AAAA   840

    Advertising Agencies—all   18,240

    Advertising Agencies—Top Execs   23,480

*Appendix **B***

How to Prepare and Use the Client Performance and Potential Profile

In Chapter 2 the Client Performance and Potential Profile was introduced. This appendix provides an in-depth discussion of the Profile and gives valuable information for your use. Each column will be discussed in turn, and the calculations and use for each will be presented.

(1) Client Name

Enter the client's name as shown on the work-in-process report, or if you are not yet automated, enter it just as you address letters to the client. You may also include the client's billing/ engagement number if you use one.

(2) Latest 12-Month Fees

Enter the total fees collected and billed during the most recent 12-month period. If you have a number of associated client entities that are more similar than different (i.e., they are within the four-digit SIC assigned to the parent entity), group these and consider them as one client.

Sort the inputs by size of total fee, from the largest to the smallest. Compute the

- Total fees for the 12-month period and list at the bottom of column (2).
- Percentage of total fee represented by each client and print out in column (3).

(3) Percentage of Total Fee

This percentage distribution is a powerful calculation. Once you have this computed, you are in position to determine your possible targeted industry market niches. I'll get to this later. For now, please read the information for the next column.

(4) Estimated Net (+) (−) Fees Next 12-Month Period

The total net dollars of revenue, plus or minus from the previous 12 months, to be derived from, or lost from, each client should be calculated and placed at the bottom of the column.

(5a) Standard Industry Code—SIC Number

Enter the four-digit SIC number for each client, using one or more of the reference sources shown in Appendix A.

(5b) Postal ZIP Code

Enter the ZIP code for each client.

(6) Quality of Client—Firm Relationship

Enter the quality of relationship for each client. Use the number 1 to represent a poor or weak relationship, and use gradations upward to the number 5, which represents the best possible relationship. If you have too many 5s you may be guilty of wishful thinking.

(7) Potential for Additional Services

The letters represent the following:

- H refers to a high potential for additional services.
- M refers to medium potential for additional services.
- L refers to a low to nonexistent potential for additional services.
- Short-term means within 12 months.
- Long-term means beyond 12 months.

(8) Client Classification

- M refers to a Mega client.
- K refers to a Key client.
- A refers to an A client.
- U refers to an Unknown client.
- B refers to a B client.
- C refers to a marginal or undesirable client.
- D refers to an undesirable client.

(9) Target Category

- O refers to a target of opportunity.
- A refers to a target of attention.
- C refers to a target of concern.

Congratulations. You now have the basic inputs for doing a marketing-centered analysis of your profile. Let's look at some additional calculations you can make.

1. Compute the total dollar value and percentage of fees within each SIC code and arrange them from largest to smallest. You can now identify your current primary and secondary industry concentrations. A primary industry has a relatively large percentage of total fees. A secondary industry has a relatively small percentage of total fees.

2. Compute the total net additional fees within each SIC code and arrange them from largest to smallest. You can now identify your estimated fastest growing industries during the next period.

Now let's look at one more "cut" you can make with your profile data:

The number of targets within each category for your primary industries can be revealing. You may find a paradox: An industry is estimated to represent large additional growth of service opportunities, but at the same time the number of targets of concern is growing.

Appendix **C**

Preparing Engagement Letters

Executive Summary

The primary advantage of a well-conceived engagement letter is that it commits to writing the agreed-on arrangements of the engagement, greatly reducing the possibility of future misunderstanding because it clarifies mutual responsibilities.

The engagement letter, as a minimum, should define the scope of the work your firm undertakes to do, the preparatory work to be done by the client's staff, the timing of the work, and fee and payment arrangements.

This appendix will present everything you need to know to prepare effective engagement letters, and will present a standard format letter you can use.

Standards of Performance

1. *No surprises.* When the client reads the letter, she should not ask herself, "I wonder what I'm going to find in here?" but "I know what's in here and I wonder how they will convey the message?"

2. *Letter is designed for the particular engagement.* It's true that approximately 70–80 percent of the material included in the typical engagement is recurring in nature. It's the 20–30 percent of the client-specific materials that need to be clearly articulated.

3. *Same level of professional care as reports and other deliverables.* The letter is a sample of the firm's deliverables and as such reflects the same level of quality as the engagement-related deliverables. Specifically, the names and title of the key client contact(s) should be properly spelled. In addition, there should be no spelling or grammatical errors, typos, or anything that suggests lack of attention and devotion to quality.

Purposes

1. *To avoid or minimize misunderstanding.* Since the client is not an expert in your field of service, it's your responsibility to be explicit in describing the scope and limitations of the engagement.

2. *To reduce any "expectations gap" on the part of the client.* During the new business discussion, it is easy to suggest benefits that could be derived from the type of work you are able to perform for your clients. The client may listen through the filter of "I really want that result" and miss the details you have attempted to negotiate for this particular engagement.

3. *To awaken the client to a realization of the practical business aspects of his relationship with the firm.* The letter is a convenient forum and vehicle for mentioning the necessity of fees being paid on a timely

basis, and that they depend on the actions of the client's people as well.

Major Elements in the Engagement Letter

1. *The key client contact person.* The engagement letter should be addressed to the person who has hired your firm, who has the authority to sign the letter and authorize payment of your invoices. If you were selected by the stockholders or the board of directors, you should address the letter to the chairperson of the board with a copy to your primary ongoing client contact person. If the arrangement was made by a corporate officer or individual business owner, the letter should be addressed to him or her.

2. *The purpose and scope of the engagement.* The scope element should include a discussion of the limitations or boundaries—what you will and will not do, prepare, and deliver. Included in this section of the letter may also be a mention of the technology you will employ in doing the engagement.

3. *Preparatory work to be done by the client.* This is an essential part of the letter. In attempting to hold down fees and to do as good a job as possible within the agreed-on time period, it's essential that the client's staff do and prepare those things that pave

the way for you and provide you with a firm foundation on which to construct the engagement results.

4. *The timing of the engagement.* Included in this element are the start and stop dates. Also include regularly scheduled progress review meetings.

5. *Fee and payment arrangements.* This element should be a clear statement about the basis for the fee, the method you will use in billing the client, and if appropriate, your expectation about when you receive the payment.

6. *Approval of the client.* Provide space at the bottom of the letter for an approval signature and date. A short sentence should ask for an approval signature.

Here is a shell of an engagement letter you can use in your practice.

SAMPLE FORMAT OF AN ENGAGEMENT LETTER

[*Letterhead*]

[Inside Address]

Dear _____:

This letter is to confirm our arrangements for _____. This letter describes the objectives and scope of the engagement, and outlines arrangements for staffing, reporting, expected time frame, and engagement fees.

OBJECTIVES

The objectives of this engagement will be to:

[*List*]

ENGAGEMENT APPROACH AND SCOPE

The approach that we will follow and the scope of this engagement is discussed below:

[*List*]

REPORTING

We will remain in close contact with you throughout the engagement. Progress meetings will be held [_____]. At the conclusion of the engagement, you will receive [_____].

STAFFING, TIMING, AND FEES

This work will be conducted by [name], [title]. She will be supervised by [name], [title] and me.

Our fees are based on the time actually invested in the engagement at our standard billing rates. We estimate our fees for this work will be approximately $_____. If it becomes apparent during the engagement that our fees will vary materially from this estimate, we will notify you before proceeding. Our policy is to invoice monthly as the work proceeds, and we expect payment within 30 to 45 days upon your receipt of the invoice.

We plan to start work on [_____], and to have it completed by [_____].

Please call if you have any questions about any aspect of this engagement. If this letter is in agreement with your understanding of our arrangements, please sign the enclosed copy and return it to us. We are looking forward to working with you on this engagement.

Sincerely yours,

Accepted By:

_____

_____, 19_____

GLOSSARY

"A" client   good clients you hope will develop into a key client. They pay their fees and are receptive to additional service discussions.

AIDA process   creating a favorable awareness, sharing information to develop an interest in seeing you, conducting need-driven discussions, and building a desire to proceed to action.

"B" client   your bread and butter clients. They pay their bills, but do not represent much potential for good fee growth.

"C" client   those who seek discounts and additional free services and are frequently slow in paying your invoices.

Client-centered marketing   the continuing process of developing and enhancing relationships with clients and other receptive people who are or can be useful to you in using, retaining, and referring you and your services.

Client referral   an existing client's providing you with leads or introductions, or vouching for you.

Comfort zone   the range of effective, self-initiated behavior in an activity area; the area of professional behavior where one is productive, confident, and forthright in one's communications and actions.

"D" client   your troublesome clients; the ones you wish you had not accepted.

Decision-making unit   the members of the client's organization who are involved in the purchase and use of your solution program.

Industry   all clients, prospective clients, and suspects in your practice area having the same four-digit SIC number.

Integrity   an unfailing consistency between what you promised and what you deliver.

Key client   one that makes referrals in your behalf, has a strong potential for fee growth, and is receptive to additional constructive service discussions.

Leveraging   concentrating on the smallest number of clients, prospects, niches, and targets that will produce the largest amount of profitable revenue; a multiplier of activity that produces a "cascade" effect of results.

Market the postal ZIP codes in your practice area for a specific SIC; a defined geographical area.

Mega client one with such fee magnitude that you can't afford to lose the relationship.

Need a generic term referring to an existing unwanted situation, a desired situation wanted and in short supply or lacking, or a task to be completed.

New business discussions the face-to-face meetings with prospective clients to define the existing and desired situations as well as a solution program for delivering the required results.

Niche an abbreviated term for the intersection of industry and market.

NCIs non-client influentials: people in the infrastructure who can assist you in meeting your marketing objectives and goals.

PAR report a report that summarizes the problem statement, approach used by your firm, and the results achieved for a given engagement.

Potential client/suspects desirable non-client organizations possessing suspected opportunity.

Promotion the process of informing, persuading, or reminding targets of opportunity and influence about your firm's ability to meet selected needs in the niche.

Proposal a document that is designed to describe the firm's ability to perform a specific task(s). Indicates that the firm has the facilities, human resources, management experience, and track record to ensure successful project performance and completion.

Prospect a former suspect who has agreed to meet with you to discuss a need situation and has not yet purchased your proposed solution program.

Prospecting the activities involved in obtaining appointments with qualified suspects for the purpose of converting them into clients or prospects.

Referrals clients and non-clients who mention your name to others and provide you with introductions and leads to new business opportunities.

Scope the range in which the engagement will be conducted.

Services delivery program the activities and worksteps involved in delivering and installing your recommended solution program.

Services promotion program the activities and worksteps involved in bringing a need and proposed service solution program to the attention of suspects in your niche.

Standard Industrial Code (SIC) a 4-digit number assigned by the U.S. Department of Commerce to identify commercial entities.

Target niche see **Niche**

Targets of influence non-clients such as attorneys and bankers with whom you do not yet have a referral relationship.

Targets of opportunity existing clients with needs and budget, prospective clients, and suspects in your niche.

Value-added service solution service deliverables/products and activities that (1) fully create the desired/required future situation within the agreed-to time and dollar budget and (2) exceeds expectations.

INDEX

Index